t₂

The
OUTDOOR SURVIVAL
Handbook

DAVID PLATTEN

DAVID & CHARLES
Newton Abbot London North Pomfret (Vt)

British Library Cataloguing in Publication Data

Platten, David
  The outdoor survival handbook.
  1. Survival (after airplane accidents,
  shipwrecks, etc.) 2. Outdoor life – Safety
  measures
  I. Title
  613.6'9   TL553.7

  ISBN 0–7153–7793–0

Library of Congress Catalog Card Number 78–75252

Typeset by Northern Phototypesetting Company, Bolton
Printed in Great Britain by
Redwood Burn Limited, Trowbridge & Esher
for David & Charles (Publishers) Limited
Brunel House Newton Abbot Devon

Published in the United States of America
by David & Charles Inc.
North Pomfret Vermont 05053 USA

Contents

Introduction

Far below you on the crisp snow, the tiny coloured wedges of the tents are perched on the lip of the bank overlooking the stream. The two orange Vango Mk IIIs and the bright red Tunnel tent punctuate the greens, tans and chocolates of the Ultimates, the Buktas, the Saunders; and the blue of your own new Marechal fills you with that same feeling of satisfaction as when you donned your first pair of proper walking boots, or packed your first real rucksack.

Turning, you look upwards, past the woolly hats and anoraks of your companions, to the skyline. Rocks, apparently frozen in the act of tumbling, are outlined crisp against a sky the colour and texture of talcum powder. Your inside curls up a little with excitement. Somewhere beyond that boulder slope, where the path is already marked by the feet of walkers even earlier in the day, winding from side to side and up over the rim of the valley, lies the Pennine Way.

You step upwards, prodding the ferrule of your borrowed ice-axe rather self-consciously into the snow. Not so very long ago, you thought ice-axes were for Alpinists, but yesterday's instruction in fall-arrest techniques, down on the lower slopes, has made you realize their place on wintry British hills as well. The fact that everybody in the party carries one is just another indication of how thoroughly you've all prepared.

This expedition is the reward of much preparation and practice: nights under summer stars, slogs across the moors in mist and rain, week-ends in camp, learning how to live comfortably, and marathon walks over half a dozen tors in a day; evenings spent with map and compass, planning routes; equipment lists and trips to the camping shops; cleaning gear, checking, adjusting, packing. And here you are, with Crowden Brook below you, the whole plateau of Kinder Scout at your feet. Next time – Snowdonia? Scotland? Somewhere foreign?

There's no end to the scope. Organized groups like this one? Week-ends of backpacking with friends? Days out on the hills?

Whatever you do, there will be the satisfaction of doing well something you're good at, the sense of achievement on winning a challenge, the excitement of meeting – and coping with – the unexpected, the freedom of being self-sufficient. Expeditioning is all of that. It is making your own adventure. This book sets out to show you how.

I am indebted to all those friends who have helped and encouraged me in the preparation of this book; in particular to David Evans, Derek and Christine Dowson and all members of the Outlook Expedition Club of Wadebridge School. I am also deeply grateful to my wife, Genny, whose patience extends even to letting me pitch my new tents on the living room floor.

David Platten

1 Basic Equipment

Feet

The first two essential pieces of equipment are your own feet. Take off your shoes and socks and look hard at what you see. There should be no bumps, corns, sore spots or callouses. The places to look at with special care are the backs of the heels, the ball of the foot and the outer sides of the big and little toes. Nails should be short; otherwise not only can they wear through your socks but, when going downhill, the foot drives them up against the toe of the boot and the resulting pressure soon becomes very painful. Nails and skin should both be kept spotlessly clean. Dirt clogs pores, causes chafe, leads to blisters and sometimes infection.

If your feet are not in good condition a visit to the chiropodist is advisable. If you're just not sure, go anyway; most people's feet are in a shocking state. In any case, a full pedicure is an experience not to be missed. You come out walking on air.

Meanwhile, you can do a lot yourself to brace up sagging feet. Walking around the house barefoot helps to strengthen skin and bone structure; bathing them in surgical spirit helps most people's feet to harden, and swabbing them with TCP or Dettol usually takes care of any minor irritation. Sufferers from Athlete's Foot will know all too well the difficulty of clearing such infections, but a solution of 3 per cent Salycylic Acid in surgical spirit, which any chemist should be able to make up for you, is wonderfully efficient. If your feet tend to sweat a lot, then regular use of a medicated foot powder, such as Tineafax or Tinaderm, will help. And, whether your feet sweat or not, a clean pair of socks every day will do as much as anything to keep them in good condition.

Socks

Socks are the next item on the essential kit list. There are two possibilities here. The first is a single pair of thick, high quality woollen socks, preferably with what is called a loop pile, for softness. Many socks of this type have some nylon content to improve resistance to wear. A small quantity of nylon – say, 25 per cent – is acceptable. The second possibility is a thin pair of fine wool socks next to the skin with a pair of coarser socks, perhaps even natural oiled wool, over the top.

Unlike man-made fibres, wool can absorb up to 37 per cent of its own weight in water without even feeling wet. Even the very best boots are rarely fully waterproof and in any case your feet will sweat, so dampness is unavoidable. Wool helps to mitigate the effects. Apart from this, natural wool possesses chemical properties which result in it actually generating heat as it dries – for example, in the warmth from your body. The old Scottish Highlanders weren't just showing off when they soaked their woollen plaids in the burn before wrapping themselves up in them to sleep!

Boots

There are dozens of reputable makes of boot, each offering something special, and the more you study them the more bewildered you seem to become. An added problem is the fact that the best boots can cost as much as a good transistor radio or cassette recorder.

Don't be put off, though. You *can* walk 16km in training shoes and still be able to hobble through your front door at the finish, but try the same walk in a pair of good boots and you will end the day wishing it were just beginning. First, be strict with yourself. If your feet have really stopped growing, spend every penny you can scrape together on a high quality pair. Don't be tempted to keep money back for other gear; that can come later. If your feet have not stopped growing, you may, with caution, buy cheaper boots since you will have grown out of them before they fall apart.

Whatever you buy, it must have a strongly reinforced toe; rough ground is hardest on the front end of a boot. The sole must be thick and heavily cleated, like a tyre tread, to give grip on slippery surfaces. The most popular type of sole is the Vibram, which comes in several different grades, all of which are good, but see page 40 for one drawback. The lacing system, whether hook, ring or eyelet, must be strong. It's not that you are going to lace the boots up so very tightly, but as you walk over uneven ground the boot rolls and flexes and this puts a considerable strain on the laces.

Fig. 1 Walking boots: one-piece upper, Vibram-type sole and bellows tongue are most important features. Speed-hook lacing, as illustrated, wears out laces quickly. Check condition frequently.

At the lower end of the scale come ordinary working boots such as those made by Tuf. These are not specialist walking boots but, with care in fitting, they make a reasonable first boot and are well made for their class.

Next come the cheaper, purpose-built walking boots, usually imported from Eastern Europe. These are quite good value and begin to feature the characteristics of the more expensive types:

hook lacing, which is easy to operate; a bellows tongue which, being attached to the boot right along both of its sides, is more waterproof than the conventional sort; and a padded ankle cuff which not only makes for increased comfort but helps to prevent stones and other rubbish from entering the top of the boot. For very little more money you can obtain specialist boots from reputable manufacturers. The Boylan Scrambler and Pindisports Wienerwald are both examples of good budget boots for the serious beginner.

If you can afford to go one step higher you can obtain excellent boots with the more sophisticated qualities you are aiming for. Such boots will be made from full grain, unsplit leather; they will have a one piece upper with a minimum of exposed stitching to rot and let in water; a full leather lining which insulates your feet but allows them to breathe; extra sole thickness; and some partial stiffening of heel and instep to provide more support on rough ground. Boots such as the Scarpa Trento, the Dolomite Vetta and the Boylan Backpacker fall into this class. There are many others in this range, and more again at a higher price still, but don't go too far. Full-weight mountain boots are too stiff and heavy for comfortable walking. As a rough guide, you should go for boots that weigh between 1·5 and 2kg per pair.

If you are buying boots by post include with your order an outline of both your feet wearing walking socks, and when the boots arrive be most particular about the fit. Don't hesitate to return them for exchange if you are in the least bit doubtful. Most firms insist that you include the carriage cost of the replacement when you return them, and this can add appreciably to the cost of an already expensive item. So really, it is best to buy your boots in person. A good shop will be staffed by experts whose advice is to be trusted, but there are some checks you can do yourself to ensure a good fit. With the boot unlaced and the foot pushed well forward, it should just be possible to slip a finger down the back of the heel inside the boot. When the laces are firmly fastened, this slackness should be taken up. Tap the toe of the boot gently against a wall or on to the floor; your foot should scarcely move inside. Try standing on tip-toe, keeping your back straight. If the boot won't let you do this at all it is too stiff, but make allowances for the fact that the leather will soften with use. More importantly, check when in this position for any pinching over the top of your foot, or any sagging at the side of the boot.

Finally, buy a tin of Hydrolan, Wetprufe, or a similar leather dressing. Boots are expensive and, in the last resort, are your life support system. They deserve to be looked after. Every other day rub a thin coat of dressing into the leather; allowing forty-eight hours between coats ensures that they are well impregnated. If you wear the boots around the house during this time, the flexing of the leather as you move will aid the process, and this will also help the boots to get to know your feet. Too much of any dressing will make the leather over-soft and the boots become floppy, so after four or five coats you can stop the treatment, giving them a good polishing after each time you've used them, and the occasional light dressing when they appear to be going dry. Traditional Dubbin, incidentally, has a reputation for rotting the stitching.

After about ten days you can use the boots on the first short walk – don't worry about blisters. If feet, socks and boots are properly matched and maintained blisters very rarely happen. How to treat them if they do occur is covered on page 124.

Body clothing

The function of clothing is to insulate. Well-chosen hiking clothes will maintain your body at a reasonable temperature, whatever the weather. Insulation is achieved by trapping air at body temperature in layers of porous clothing, and stopping the wind from blowing it away. Ideally your clothes should insulate from heat as well as cold, but in practice this is very difficult. When walking over rough terrain, uphill, carrying packs, working hard, it's much easier to get too warm than too cold! The best you can do is to work on the principle that you can always strip off what you're wearing, but you can't put on what you don't have with you.

Owing to the fact that out in the country the weather is

always cooler than you think it's going to be – and can turn nasty in the time it takes to wish you had an extra sweater – you ought to be wearing all of the following: cellular underwear – long in winter, short in summer; warm trousers; a pure wool sweater, preferably polo-necked; and a flannel shirt or a windcheater. In addition you should carry waterproof outer clothing and a reserve of warm wear. All of these items can be bought, specially designed for the purpose, from good camping shops. However, there are cheaper, non-specialist garments on the market which, carefully chosen, do the job just as well.

An ordinary sweater worn next to the skin is as effective as a fish-net vest. It separates the rest of your clothing from your body, thus trapping a layer of warm air. The lower half of the body can be protected in summer by games shorts under your trousers and in winter by flannelette pyjamas or even a thickish pair of women's tights. There is no real substitute for the pure wool sweater – we have already seen what wool can do – and most families can produce at least one, but if you do have to buy it, you can always wear it at other times. It need not be a thick one; my favourite was knitted for me out of baby wool and is more than adequate.

With regard to trousers and windcheaters, there are various possibilities. For summer walking, a track suit is usually sufficient – and, again, it can be used on other occasions. However, when you come to spend the night out, the track suit has other jobs to do. It doubles as dry clothing and sleeping suit.

More suitable for day-time clothing, and even cheaper, is a pair of army surplus worsted, or even serge, trousers and an army flannel combat shirt. The great advantage of these, apart from their price, is the fact that the army believes in practicability rather than fashion. The trousers are usually full in the seat, as good backpacking trousers should be, to allow ease of movement. The bottoms are narrow and fit neatly over the boot cuff. As a bonus, they are very strongly made and seem to have exceptionally large pockets. Much the same considerations apply to army shirts, the bonuses here being the epaulettes so useful for holding hat and gloves, and the securely buttoned breast-pockets for carrying personal odds and ends.

Widely flared trousers are definitely out for serious walking. They flap around, catch on obstructions, and soon get soaked and filthy. Thin denim jeans of any style are always unsuitable since they offer virtually no insulation or resistance to wind. They should be worn only in the warmest of weather, changes in which are unlikely, and only if you have a good reserve of more efficient clothing with you. The same limitations, of course, apply to T-shirts and cotton singlets.

Shell clothing

The cheapest way of keeping the rain off is to buy a large polythene bag, big enough to go over your head and pack and reach down to your knees. Cut a hole for your face, and there you have it. It's not ideal but it will serve for the unexpected shower on a one-day trek in summer, and it's more efficient than a plastic mac.

If you are going to buy proper shell clothing, which – as its name implies – is a fully protective suit, it is not worth buying cheap items. Unless the nylon fabric of which these garments are usually made is proofed with polyurethane or neoprene it is not waterproof and no amount of silicone spraying from handy aerosols will make it so. Even proofed garments are little use if they are of the lightest weight, which the cheap ones usually are. The proofing is efficient enough when new but soon breaks down under the stress of being chafed by rucksack straps, sat on, stuffed in and pulled out from under the top flap of your pack, and so on.

A more robust investment is the 135g or 165g PU coated nylon garment, such as the G & H Cagjac. Even stronger is neoprene-coated nylon. It usually weighs around 270g per metre and garments of this material can be heavy to carry around when you're not wearing them. Perhaps a good compromise is the 135g neoprene/nylon as used, for example, in the Henri Lloyd Fitzroy jacket.

As far as design is concerned, the most popular garment is the cagoule which is basically a knee-length smock with a hood.

There are various refinements such as neck gussets closed by a zip, storm cuffs or velcro fasteners to seal the ends of the sleeves around the wrists in bad weather, and draw-cords at hem and hood. All of these you pay for, and all are useful, but the pull-over cagoule suffers from one overriding drawback: the inside sweats.

Actually, it's you who sweat. When your body is at work inside shell clothing, the moisture which is given off as vapour condenses on the cold inner surface of the waterproof fabric. It is then soaked up by your clothes and soon you are as wet as if you wore nothing. Stripping off underneath your shell clothing to stay cool is not always the answer – we have already talked about the need for insulation.

The cure for condensation is ventilation. A cagoule-style jacket with a full-length zip, usually protected from the weather by a velcro or stud-fastened flap, allows you to open it right up when the wind and rain are at your back. The better ones are usually fitted with a two-way zip which can be opened at either end so that you can vent the bottom or the top. Since the crotch, head and neck are three zones of greatest heat loss on the body, it makes sense to be able to ventilate these areas when feeling warm. I have even known broad-minded backpackers wander around with their flies undone!

By itself, the cagoule does not offer full protection from rain or wind. You can lose valuable body heat as the wind whips through your unprotected trousers. Rain, meanwhile, drips steadily from the hem of your jacket, soaks your knees, trickles down your shins and into your boots. Overtrousers are essential.

Ventilation is even more important with these relatively close-fitting garments. To my mind, the only truly practical design for overtrousers is that which incorporates a full length, two-way zip up the inside leg. Apart from making ventilation very easy, the legs can be rolled up and tucked into the waistband when the sun shines between the showers, so that you don't get the insides muddy when pulling them on and off over your boots. Troll Overtrollies use this system – and they are made from 115g neoprene/nylon, with reinforced seat and knees.

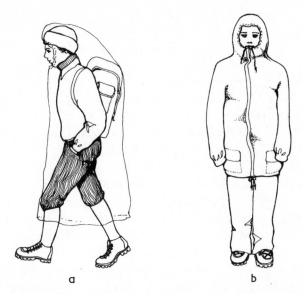

Fig. 2   Shell clothing: (a) cheap and effective, plastic bag with face hole cut in front; (b) more convenient to walk in, cagoule-style jacket and overtrousers.

Knee-length gaiters are a useful extra though not absolutely essential. They protect the bottoms of your trouser-legs from dirt, and from damage by catching on obstructions; they help to prevent rubbish, water and snow from entering the top of the boot, and offer some protection from rain if worn with a knee-length cagoule. Nylon ones are more waterproof than canvas, but are subject to condensation, so canvas is better if you're going to be wearing them all the time.

Warm wear

A woollen hat, preferably a balaclava, gloves, preferably mittens, and a spare sweater are the final items of clothing on the basic list.

Brushed Scotch wool balaclavas are available from camping shops; army surplus stores are another source of reasonable hats, or you can use a home-knitted one. Mittens – warmer than gloves – soon get soggy when it's raining, as the water drips off your sleeves, but the oiled wool variety are fairly weather-resistant, or you can buy waterproof overmitts. Karrimor and Helly Hansen also produce a PU-coated nylon mitt with a warm fibre lining.

Home-knitted woollen clothes can be made water-resistant by rubbing lanolin into them. If you can't obtain pure lanolon, Hydrolan leather dressing, used sparingly, will do at a pinch. If mittens or balaclavas are being home-knitted, make them, say, 10cm longer in the wrist and neck than most patterns suggest, since these areas also radiate a lot of body heat.

The spare sweater, carried as reserve insulation or for preventing yourself from becoming chilled when you stop for a rest, should ideally be of wool, but there are alternatives to this garment. For the wealthy, a down or dacron-filled jacket is a good investment. When not in use, these garments compress very small but swell out agàin ('lofting' is the technical term) to provide marvellous insulation. If you are going to do much winter walking, you should seriously consider buying one of these. They are all smart enough to be used as ordinary warm casual wear, which makes them better value than they seem at first. The relative merits of down and dacron are discussed on page 76. Suffice it to say here that dacron will retain most of its insulation when it is wet, and will dry much more quickly than down. Our wet/cold British weather makes dacron a serious proposition with regard to duvets, as these garments are called.

More versatile as an item of warm wear is the fibre-pile jacket. This is made from something similar but superior to nylon 'fur' fabric, with the 'fur' inside providing a layer of warm air around the body. These garments are not really windproof, so the insulation is lost in wild weather unless you wear shell clothing over them. Nevertheless, they're very good value. They cost no more than a good wool sweater, are just as smart, and can be bought with matching trousers to make a really warm suit. Many climbers and ramblers are actually using these as basic walking wear, and they can also be used as a winter-time sleeping suit. Helly Hansen, Insulata, Javelin and North Cape are the best known. Insulata are very reasonably priced and use more resin in the bonding of their fabric than do the others. This makes it less prone to piling (forming little balls of fluff on the surface). They produce a zipped jacket, with hood and pockets which make it particularly useful. A cheap, but much heavier alternative is RAF thermal underwear, made from a similar fabric and – again – obtainable from government surplus stores.

Now you are completely clothed. The elements can do what they will. But, you are not yet quite fully equipped for walking. A few more small items remain.

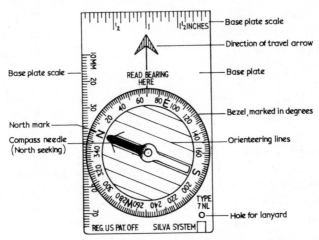

Fig. 3   The Silva compass: type 7 NL.

Compass, watch and whistle

The first of these is a compass, and it is generally accepted that the combined compass/protractor is the most useful. With this you can not only take bearings and find out which way you are walking, but you can lay off courses on the map and measure distances. Silva manufacture a complete range, types 3 and 7 being the most popular. Type 7 differs from type 3 in having a shorter protractor plate which might conceivably affect accuracy when working with it on the map. Instructions on use are included with every compass, and further explanations may be found on pages 25–7, 43–5, and 64.

The second item is a reliable watch. Apart from allowing you to keep an eye on your schedule as you walk, it enables you to

calculate your speed; or, given your speed, you can work out
how far you've travelled. Do check, before you set off, though,
that it's fully wound.

The whistle is an item you should always have, but shouldn't
ever use except in an emergency when you really do need to
summon help. The recognized international distress signal is
one blast every ten seconds for a minute, followed by a minute's
silence while you listen for the reply, which is one blast every
twenty seconds in alternate minutes. However, any
experienced walker who hears *any* sort of whistle in wild
country may well assume that there's an emergency at hand
and react accordingly, so don't go blowing off just for the fun of
it.

Space blanket

This is also a piece of emergency equipment which no
responsible walker would leave behind, and there are two,
perhaps three, possibilities here. Space blankets are made from
a very thin, light, strong plastic which is metallized to produce
a surface which reflects heat, light and radar. They're so thin
that you can see through them, but they will reflect 90 per cent
of your body heat back at you. In an emergency, wrapping
yourself up in one of these can save your life.

Purpose-built space blankets weight only about 56g and fold
very small. You can fit one into a shirt pocket. Theoretically
they are expendable – use once and throw away. One would
hope that you don't intend to make a habit of having to use it, so
this is no real drawback. However, if they're treated with care
and painstakingly refolded, they can be saved for another time.
On the occasions when I have been involved with any sort of
casualty – even a minor one – my first reaction has been to
produce a space blanket. Consequently, in the first-aid kit that
I carry when I'm taking large groups out, I carry one used and
one unused space blanket.

The better of the other two possibilities is a sportsman's
blanket. This is a sturdy, indefinitely reusable groundsheet
with the same reflective qualities. Apart from its emergency

value, it makes a seating mat when stopping for lunch, a warmth reflecting wind-break on the beach, an insulating ground cloth for your tent, or, with its silver side outwards, it can provide cool shade on a hot day. It is heavier and bulkier than a space blanket, but can still be carried in the side pocket of a rucksack. It is, of course, more expensive than a lightweight space blanket but, being more versatile, it is to my mind a better investment.

If your budget is really tight then a bivvy bag is better than nothing. This is simply a large polythene bag big enough for one, or even two, people to crawl into, and stout enough not to cling to their faces and suffocate them. The cheapest version is just a sheet of builder's polythene. A piece about 2·5m square is the most useful size. However, you can purchase a bag which is bright orange and makes a highly visible target for would-be rescuers, and is still quite inexpensive.

Problem pack

Next comes an item which deserves special attention. It will cost you practically nothing, since you make it yourself – and it's great fun to put together. Unlike the whistle or the lightweight space blanket, some of its ingredients you may use quite frequently.

The first step is to obtain one of the rectangular type of 50g tobacco tin, or something similar. Using a razor-blade scrape the markings off the lid and shine it up with metal polish; you now have a signalling mirror. Inside – and this takes patience and ingenuity – fit a 3m roll of gauze bandage; a roll of surgical tape such as Micropore, which is lighter and more versatile than elastic bandage; a little sachet of Savlon cream; four or five pain-killing tablets, such as Codis, which come in handy foil strips; a new razor-blade in its waxed paper envelope; 30sq cm of aluminium baking foil; a nightlight candle; a book of matches; an Oxo cube; and as many glucose tablets as you can find room for. These are the items you hope not to use. How you do so if you have to is covered in various parts of this book, particularly in Chapter 8.

In addition, a large safety pin, a needle and about 3m of strong thread – fishing line is good if you have a large-eyed needle – a couple of metres of thin wire, such as 15-amp fuse wire, and a 7cm hardened steel masonry nail have a variety of uses in making running repairs and improvising gadgets. It's tricky getting it all in, but it does fit! I manage to include even a packet of salt and a couple of indigestion tablets (in case my friends can't cook). One companion I walk with seals his tin with electrician's PVC insulating tape which on one occasion, reused, proved useful for repairing my air-bed when he'd stuck his knife through it!

Since your problem pack already contains glucose and Oxo cube, the need for a packet of emergency food is not as great as it might otherwise be. However, in winter, or on longer treks, it's worth taking something extra. The most useful ration would be a 50g bar of fruit and nut milk chocolate, a 50g block of brown Kendal Mint Cake, and a small Tupperware container or non-glass screw-cap jar of invalid food, such as Complan which now comes in a variety of flavours. This last may be made up with water into a hot drink. It's highly nutritious and easily digestible. All this is in addition to your normal day's food, of course, and should not under any circumstances be touched, other than in a real emergency. Keep them in a sealed packet to reduce the temptation.

I doubt very much the value of taking along any of the little solid fuel stoves on the market, even for an emergency, and certainly not for the routine heating of a midday drink. They're expensive to run and very slow to cook on. Lighting fires on the trail is not to be encouraged, but in an emergency it's the obvious morale booster, as well as a source of heat and light. On a day-trek, a good large vacuum flask is as useful as anything.

If you wish to carry a stove and are thinking of buying camping equipment as well as personal gear, turn to page 82. There are numerous choices, but for day-treks the common little Camping Gaz stove will do. Even cheaper, and to my mind more effective, is the Express Picnic meths burner, obtainable from most hardware stores.

Day packs

The final item of personal gear which it is worth buying for yourself is a cheap, light, nylon day sack. These little rucksacks can be obtained almost anywhere. The only types to avoid are those with lots of side pockets, which are unnecessary on a day sack and make it less suitable for its other use.

On extended expeditions the same sack can be stowed inside your proper pack as a ditty-bag in which to keep odds and ends tidily. For short trips away from a standing camp, you then have a day sack ready and waiting. It's amazing how many packets of crisps and cans of suitable refreshment you can bring back to camp in one of these when you're planning a cosy evening!

With all this gear acquired, you are now equipped for a day-trek in most conditions. For the complete novice, day-treks are an essential introduction to the art of expeditioning. Even for the more experienced, they provide valuable opportunities for developing their skills. So, before we consider any more equipment, let's look at what's involved in going on a day-trek.

2 Making Ready

Attitudes

Lots of people go for walks – and, surprisingly, most of them come back. You can meet the flip-flop brigades toiling up Snowdon, Helvellyn, Ben Nevis or the first 5km of the Pennine Way on any bank holiday.

More people than care to admit it are willing to set out for the day ill-prepared because they believe they would feel embarrassed at being apparently over-dressed in contrast to the crowds. In any case, the mountains don't look very forbidding when the path has been stamped into a pedestrian highway, and the Coca Cola cans and orange peel are glinting in the sunshine all the way to the top. But stop to think; what happens when the mist comes down, or when the wind pipes up and the temperature drops by twenty degrees?

Actually, the general public is beginning to learn. Thanks to the vigilance of wardens and rangers, the publicity campaigns for safety and the country code, and the example set by people like yourself, the majority of those whom you'll meet on the trail will recognize you as someone who knows what he's doing. This means, of course, that you have a responisbility not only to yourself – many people resent being told that anyway – and not only to the almost incredibly dedicated mountain-rescue teams who will risk their lives to haul you out of any jam which your own stupidity may have got you into, but also to those other thousands who know they aren't doing things properly, and are secretly watching you to see what they can learn.

Taking CARE

CARE is the expeditioner's watchword. The C stands for *Companions*. Until you're an expert, at any rate, you should *never* venture alone on a trip. Three should really be regarded as a minimum, and four is ideal. Should there be an accident, one can stay with the casualty and the other two, giving each other moral support, can fetch help. The A stands for Advice. Local advice on conditions, the suitability of your route, the weather forecast, the best place to camp, and so on, should be sought and followed. R is for Resolution. Resolve that you will not make the same mistakes as last time, that you will think before acting, that you will make an effort to improve your techniques. Resolution can also mean having the guts to carry on when you feel like chucking it all in and going home – but don't try and be a hero yet! The E, of course, refers to Equipment. We have already discussed the virtues of good equipment, but there is one other point worth making. It is the last element in the list. Even the best pieces of equipment are no more than tools, like footballs or cricket bats. The team's skill wins the game.

The other difference between expeditioners and mere walkers is that expeditioners have a sense of purpose. The purpose needn't be very formal; admiring the scenery can be a sufficient excuse for going out. Apart from this, you may be interested in photography, wild-life spotting, botany, geology, navigation, physical fitness; or you may have some particular project in hand, ranging from a survey of industrial archaeology along the West Country coastal path to bagging all 280 Scottish Munroes inside twelve months. (Now there's a challenge!) The important thing is that you should make it a deliberate policy to follow some purpose.

Of course, the purpose will vary with the terrain. The dedicated fell runner will find less challenge on the South Downs Way than in the Lake District, but the variations are more subtle than that. A detailed study of the area beforehand should reveal the interests most appropriate to it, and this is where we start with the planning of our first day-trek.

Maps

It all begins with the map. Not only will it show you the way; it can give you a wealth of information about the area. Things like the steepness of the route are obvious from the spacing of the contour lines. Equally obvious are whether the area is wooded or not, whether the ground is marshy, even whether the going will be made difficult by boulder fields, rock outcrops and streams. Closer examination will reveal more subtle details. The number of view points marked on any given area of a tourist map will tell you, with surprising accuracy, the number of people you can expect to see around; the closeness of the farm houses will tell you how intensively cultivated the area is; the number and depth of the valleys will even tell you something about the nature of the rock over which you are to travel. To the experienced expeditioner, a map looks like a stereoscopic photograph, taken from the air.

The maps to go for are the Ordnance Survey 1:25,000 scale second series. These are the product of the most recent surveys and, with a scale of about 2½in to the mile, they show every detail. The only snag is that large areas of the country are not yet covered by them. The 1:25,000 first series maps aren't so good. The surveys on which they're based were last fully revised in 1905 and even partial revision has left them misleading in places. Some of the more popular areas of the country, like the national parks, are served by Outdoor Leisure maps, based on the 1:25,000 first series, but containing much additional information which really does make them useful.

Coming a very close second – and in fact preferred by many backpackers because they show a far greater area on one sheet – are the 1:50,000 scale maps, which are also the product of recent surveys. These are the successors to the old 1in OS maps, and the slight increase in scale makes a great deal of difference.

It really depends on how difficult a route you wish to plan, how accurately you need to navigate it, or how much detail you find interesting. Perhaps the ideal arrangement is to buy a 1:50,000 sheet of the general area, and the relevant 1:25,000 sheets – first or second series – to cover the actual route. You can then spend happy hours transferring information from one to the other.

I will assume that you have already mastered the rudiments of map reading. You should, for example, already be able to work out a six-figure grid reference; know what contour lines are; and recognize symbols used on the map to represent features on the ground. If all this is still beyond you, don't despair. Just by looking at the map, and reading all the information in the margin, you will find out about the details above. However, check with an expert, or preferably seek proper instruction. School teachers, Scout and Guide leaders, a local rambling club – any of these would be able to help.

Route cards

Given a basic knowledge of map work, it needs only practice to turn it into map craft – the ability to read a map like an experienced expeditioner. The most efficient way to practise is to draw up and fill in route cards. The route card contains all the essential information about your proposed route to enable anyone else possessing a copy to find you at any time during the trek. The route card (Fig. 6) contains even more than the essentials, but filling in every column will make you study the map closely and will very quickly teach you to find your way around it.

The need to enter two grid references in the left-hand columns may not seem apparent at first, but it does eliminate any chance of confusing the reference of the point from which you start with the point to which you're going. Believe me, I've seen it happen!

The compass course for each leg of the route is obtained simply by laying one edge of the protractor plate along the route, with the direction of travel arrow pointing the way you want to go. Ignoring the magnetic needle, turn the movable ring, or bezel, until the north mark is pointing along the north/south grid lines. Make sure it does point northwards and not south! You can now read what's called the *true bearing* of the course at the point marked on the protractor plate.

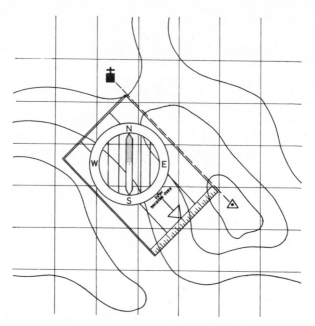

Fig. 4 Laying off a compass course: orienteering lines in compass bowl run parallel to grid lines on map when bezel is swung into position.

In the field you can ignore the difference between *true north* and *grid north*, but you should correct the *true bearing* for *variation* before entering it on the route card. *Magnetic variation* tends to fill people with alarm and despondency but it's really very simple. True north and magnetic north are actually in different places on the earth's surface, and magnetic north has a habit of moving around. At the foot of the map there is always a note which tells you how many degrees difference there were between grid and magnetic north when the map was published, and how much the difference changes each year. For example, it may say *Magnetic variation is 8° 00′ W of grid north for June 1965. Annual change 5′ E.* There are 60′ in a degree, so in 1979 magnetic north will be 6° 50′ west of grid north. For our purposes we may round this off to the nearest whole degree, which makes it 7° west. Since we are ignoring the difference between grid north and true north, all we have to do now is to add 7° to the true bearing, and we have the compass bearing.

There are various rhymes and jingles to help you remember

whether to add or subtract variation but they are usually more a source of confusion than help. If you can't remember what to do, copy the following table into the notes section of your route card:

To transfer bearings from map to route card or ground	Add westerly variation Subtract easterly variation
To transfer bearings from ground or route card to map	Subtract westerly variation Add easterly variation

If you think about this, it's obvious; and with practice it will soon become instinctive.

The next column on the route card refers to distance in kilometres. The reason for working in kilometres rather than miles is simply that the grid lines on a map are all 1km apart. It is therefore easier to estimate distances in kilometres, using the grid lines as a guide. Again, practice will make perfect. You can buy map measurers – little wheels marked with a graduated scale – but estimating the distances makes you study the map more closely and is therefore to be preferred, although, until you're good at it, you should use a measurer, or a piece of string laid along the route and compared in length with the scale marked on the map, as a final check.

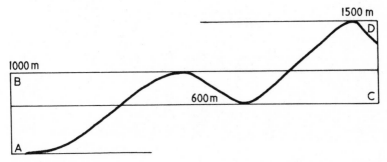

Fig. 5 Calculating height for Naismith's rule: total height gained is A–B plus C–D; height lost between B and C is ignored unless terrain is very steep and difficult.

NAME A. Walker	EXPEDITION						Day Trek: Bradford Bridge – Brown Willy Tor – Bradford Bridge	DATE 25.3.78
GRID REF ON SX15 OS 1:25,000		COURSE °C	DIST IN KMS	ASCENT	DESCENT	TIME IN '	TERRAIN	NOTES
FROM	TO							
119755	123764	045	1.0	100	–	19	From Bradford Bridge follow track to end	Bearings along paths approximate only.
125764	126768	031	0.5	–	–	8	Across open moor to junction of tracks	Times rounded up to nearest minute.
126768	133768	090	0.8	75	25	15	Track through fields to Leage Farm. Ford over stream	Phone at Bradford Bridge 119755.
133768	139777	031	1.3	50	75	22	Open moor. Past stone circle to foot bridge	
139777	147797	016	2.1	200	–	40	Open moor. Past Garrow Tor to corner of plantation	Farmcar House occupied 151798
147797	159800	065	1.1	500	75	37	Via bridge steep slope to Brown Willy Trig point	
159800	157783	155	1.8	–	500	21	Follow ridge down to Butters Tor Farm	Forecast: Scattered showers clearing from west later. Wind NW. Force 4.
157783	158762	180	2.0	–	50	30	Follow path along stream to ford	
158762	141756	239	1.8	275	125	38	Open moor to Hawks Tor Trig point	
141756	134749	221	1.0	–	225	15	Open moor to Hawks Tor Cottage and footbridge	
134749	129747	226	0.5	–	25	8	Follow track to junction with road	Lambing still in progress. Beware sheep.
129747	119755	315	1.0	–	100	15	Follow road to Bradford Bridge	
			14.9	1200	1200	274		Checkpoint 029 1247

Fig. 6 The Route Card.

The columns relating to height gained and lost are most important. Actual distance means little in wild country, and the length of a route is more usually considered in time: 4km along a level road, for example, will take you less than an hour to walk; 4km up a 450m mountainside will take you twice as long. It also takes time to lose height, but in practice this can be ignored for the purpose of timing a route.

The most useful guide to timing is Naismith's Rule, which demands that you allow 60 minutes for every 4km travelled according to the map, and 4 minutes extra for every 30m of height gained. This works out very accurately.

Having worked out the distance and the height gained you can now fill in the 'time' column. Entering the time in minutes for each leg of the route allows you to keep a check on your progress as you go. It also allows the people you will have notified before leaving, and to whom you will have given a copy of the route card, to know roughly where you are at any moment.

The column labelled 'Terrain' should contain a brief description of the ground over which you will be travelling. It need be no more, for example, than 'Fields' or 'Open moorland' but filling it in does ensure that you have looked closely at the map. Any obstacles, such as streams or boulder fields, should also be listed, and it is useful to give a name to each grid reference, such as 'Brown Willy trig point' or 'Corner of plantation'. Names like these roll off the tongue more easily when discussing the route with your companions, than do the lengthy figures of a grid reference.

Finally, the space available for notes should contain details of the weather forecast, the phone number of the people you notified before leaving, grid references of the nearest mountain-rescue posts or telephone kiosks – to save you poring over the map in moments of stress – and any special information, such as restrictions imposed by areas being closed for game shooting, army firing practice, drought control, etc.

The route card and map should be considered as inseparable. They should be with you at all times on the trail and you should understand both perfectly. So before going any further, find yourself a map – any area of reasonably wild country will do – and a compass; and then go back and read these last two sections again. When you fully understand them, you are ready to proceed with the rest of your planning.

Planning the route

The route you select for your first day-trek is best confined to established footpaths or recognized rambles. Most areas of interest to walkers are covered by guide books or leaflets of one sort or another. The walks suggested in these form a good basis from which to begin.

If your first walk is not to be in such an area, you should study the map particularly carefully. It's a good idea to follow a route you already know, but this time to do it properly; you will be surprised at how much detail you missed before.

At any rate, whether you pick a recognized ramble, a familiar route, or try following the paths through country new to you, don't be too ambitious. Keep the walk short – not more than 12km at the outside – and steer clear of any particular navigational difficulties. At this stage, rock scrambling, river fording and summit bagging are definitely out. So are striking out across trackless moor, taking short cuts down steep slopes and wandering over farmland through which there is no right of way.

If all this sounds as though your sense of adventure is being firmly squashed, don't worry. Firstly, you'll be too busy following the advice which is to come to feel the need for extra adventure; and secondly, when you have followed the advice and returned home safely, you will feel satisfied, not to say smug, knowing that you are one of the responsible ones.

Having selected your route, you should fill in two route cards and make a blank copy to take with you. One of the cards is left at your check-point. This is simply a place, for example your home, where someone agrees to wait for you, and to notify the authorities if you are overdue. Ideally, the check-point should be on the phone and you should have the number. Most mountain information centres – not to be confused with the quite different mountain-rescue centres – can usually offer this service.

The authorities to be contacted in a crisis vary from place to place. It may be the police, the coastguard, the local mountain-rescue centre, or some other special organization. However, the police, if contacted initially, will advise, and it is your job to find out and tell your check-point before you set off.

Make quite sure that your check-point understands exactly where you are going; who is going with you; what gear you are taking, including clothing; when you are setting out and when you expect to be back. In the unfortunate event of his having to contact the authorities, he will then have all the information they require, including a copy of that vital document, the route card which the authorities will ask for – and be most impressed with if he can produce it.

There is no need for your check-point to start worrying if you're ten minutes late on your estimated time of arrival. The normal period of time allowed to elapse after ETA before a party is posted as overdue is three hours. In winter or very bad weather it would be less. If the check-point does feel worried, though, it is best for him to follow his instinct and phone. The people to whom he will be passing the responsibility are more experienced in making the right decisions.

It won't be very long before you can do all this preparation the evening before you set off without batting an eyelid. At the moment, however, it probably seems like an awful lot of work. Much of the planning starts as dreaming: a few sessions with map and compass over a month of winter evenings, the odd entry on a route card, the occasional phone call or letter, and hours of discussing with your friends expeditions as ambitious as you care to imagine, as well as the trek that you're actually going to do.

Packing

The evening before the trek is the time when you really start getting ready. All gear, including clothing, should be given a quick check to ensure that it is complete and in good condition.

The full overhaul, of course, comes after you return from an expedition. What you are looking for now is any deterioration in emergency rations, any item that has got lost, and so on.

The day's food comes next. Sandwiches and fruit cake are all right but the traditional backpacker's trail ration will give you greater energy, be easier to carry, and is dietetically much better considered. It consists of cheese or tinned meat, biscuits such as crispbread or cream crackers, a handful of dried fruit – raisins, sultanas, dried apricots or pressed dates – and a touch of luxury with which to finish. This may indeed be the piece of fruit cake, or perhaps a couple of chocolate biscuits.

In addition, you should have either a vacuum flask or the ingredients for a hot drink, and a stove on which to make it. Instant soup is the obvious choice, but tea or coffee are often more appreciated. I always pack an Oxo cube with my lunch, and I usually discard it in favour of a tea-bag.

Also part of your day's rations should be a plentiful supply of trail snacks – sweets, chocolate, nuts, and so on – to nibble while on the move. It's amazing how a bite of something when you're tired can make the day seem brighter. Something cool to drink is also a good idea, especially in warm weather, but take the can and its pull-ring top home with you, please. Lemonade powder for adding to water collected in a plastic bottle en route is another possibility.

Pack your rations inside a sandwich box or a polythene bag which will hold your day's litter when you've eaten the food and keep it separate from the other items in the day pack.

Apart from the food, your day pack should contain the following: fibre-pile jacket or spare sweater; sportsman's blanket, if that is what you've opted for; shell clothing; vacuum flask or stove with fuel either in the tank or in a separate container, as appropriate; and your emergency rations packed in a sealed container. A small electric torch and cheap plastic cigarette lighter are invaluable in an emergency – the latter will be required anyway if you have a stove – and one of the party could usefully include some toilet tissue and a light trowel.

Since cheap day packs are rarely waterproof line the inside with a polythene bag. Even if the weather looks fine and settled it's worth being prepared. The order in which you fill a day sack doesn't really matter; you're carrying so little that the effect on your balance is negligible. But, for the sake of comfort, place the sweater next to your spine to make a soft pad against your back, and the shell clothing at the top so that you can reach it, if it starts raining, with the minimum of bother.

The items which should preferably be carried in your pockets are: the problem pack, lightweight space blanket, if this is your choice, trail snacks, and a small notepad. Most people like to carry a strong sheath or clasp knife, but on a day-trek one rarely needs it.

The compass should hang round your neck on a lanyard, and the whistle can be carried in the same way. If there's any metal in it, keep it away from the compass when you're using the latter or you'll upset the magnetic needle. In whichever pockets are most convenient there should be the ball-point pen and the blank route card, and some small change for phones. If you carry season tickets to National Trust properties, or identification cards of some organization, such as The Duke of Edinburgh's Award Scheme, the Scout Association or a rambling club, these can be kept handy in a wallet in a back pocket.

This leaves the map and route card. No one has yet devised a really handy way of carrying these. You need to be able to look at them at any time, but to keep them out of the way when they're not needed. You want to be able to see as much of the map as possible but without having to struggle against vast sheets of flimsy paper. And both map and route card need to be waterproofed.

Clear plastic map cases with lanyards can be bought, and are reasonably waterproof. They can be hung round your neck or slung over a shoulder like a haversack. Such a case can also be improvised from a polythene bag sealed with PVC tape (electrician's insulating tape will do). The disadvantages of these are that you seem to be forever taking out the map and refolding it to show the next stretch of the route – at which time it is unprotected and in wild weather soon gets tattered – and also that as you walk, the case flaps in the breeze, the lanyard tangles itself up with your compass and whistle, and you soon begin to feel distinctly trapped.

An alternative arrangement is to cover the map, front and back, with clear, self-adhesive plastic film, such as that made by Fablon for covering books. The route card can be treated in the same way. When not in use, map and route card can be stuffed inside your shirt, hooked over your belt, or slid into a map-sized thigh pocket on your trousers. When required, the whole map can be spread out on the ground regardless of how damp it may be or can be folded to reveal just the area required. It's quite good for sitting on as well during short rests when the ground is damp. The snags with this method are that you can drop and lose the map; the folds in it cannot really be smoothed out, which makes reading that bit of the map a little tricky, and the plastic does eventually crack.

Some people recommend chopping the map into small sheets. Don't. You should always arrange the map so that where you're standing is in the middle of the bit you're looking at, and that's much easier when you've got the whole sheet to play with.

You will have to experiment to find a system which suits you, but make a point of avoiding the most common fault of all – letting somebody else do the navigating. Everyone in the party should know exactly where he is and how he got there.

Now, at last, you're ready to go. But, having dressed and packed, spend a few minutes adjusting dress and pack straps until you're really comfortable. You should be able to move your limbs freely and the pack should stay firmly in position. Swing your arms, try a few knee bends, jog up and down on the spot. Any chafing of clothing, rattling of gear or bumping of the pack will become irritating later, so deal with it now.

3 The Day-trek

Setting off

Few of us are fortunate enough to live so near to good walking country that we can step right into it from our own front doors; and even if you're one of the lucky ones, you'll soon want to travel further afield. The chances are that, having arrived at the starting point of your trek, you are in surroundings that you've not looked at in the flesh before. Even familiar areas take on a new significance when compared with the map, so it is worth taking time at the start of your trek to get your bearings.

Check with your compass to find true north accurately, then spread your map out on the ground, turn it round so that north on map and ground coincide, and identify on it everything you can see around you. You'll find that this improves your sense of direction later in the day when you look around and see the same hills and landmarks from different angles.

Now, pause for a moment to absorb the atmosphere of the area. Listen to the sounds, look at the clouds, feel the wind. This is not just to try and cultivate the poet in you, although there's no harm in that. While you needn't try consciously to make any deductions from the atmosphere about the conditions you'll encounter, stopping long enough to take it all in does put you in tune with the environment; and if you do this regularly throughout the trek, you will find before too many expeditions are past that in fact you are developing an instinct for forecasting conditions.

The stillness and the deepening hush which settle almost imperceptibly upon the hills, the hint of tension in the air around you as you climb higher and higher towards the velvet haze above your chosen summit, can mean quite simply that you're walking into a thunderstorm. And in the mountains, that –

you'd better believe – is not to be dismissed as mere poetic fancy: it can be as dangerous as it is frightening. How to make more deliberate predictions is covered in Chapter 9.

Adjusting dress

As you set off, you will be fully clothed, even wearing your hat and gloves if it is chilly. If there's anything more in the way of wind than a gentle breeze, you will also be wearing a cagoule.

Wind is an exposure hazard not always fully appreciated. Not only does it blow away the warm air trapped in your clothing; it evaporates your body moisture and, in extreme cases, can lead to dehydration as well as hypothermia from exposure. It's worth remembering that even in calm, temperate conditions the human body can begin to show signs of dehydration after less than five hours without taking in water.

However, being over-dressed leads to excessive perspiration, and this merely aggravates the condition you're trying to avoid. In any case, the energy required to perspire is better employed in putting one foot in front of the other. So the experienced walker is forever adjusting his clothing to achieve the optimum level of ventilation and insulation.

First to be shed are hat and gloves, and it's amazing how much difference this makes. Then the cagoule is unzipped, taken off, and finally, shirt buttons undone. Letting your shirt tails and sweater hang outside your trousers increases ventilation further. Only when all this has proved insufficient should you start taking off basic clothing; and the rule here is to work from the inside out, leaving the windproof outer clothing in place. This is obviously more bother than simply peeling off a shirt, or stripping down to shorts, but the experienced walker is always extra-cautious about exposing unprotected skin.

Apart from the danger of exposure leading to hypothermia – the potentially fatal lowering of body-core temperature – there is the risk of sun or wind burn. And because the wind keeps your skin cool, you don't notice the smarting until it's too late. In high summer a small tube of sun-tan cream and a stick of lipsalve are very useful additions to the pack.

On stopping for a rest your first reaction should be to put some of the discarded clothing back on again. After toiling up a steep gradient it is tempting to stand exposed at the top, letting the cooling wind sift through your sticky clothes. Perhaps there's no harm in letting this happen for a minute or two, but be prepared to put your hat on anyway, and start getting dressed again as soon as you feel comfortable. If the weather is not warm enough for you to have shed any clothing, you should resort to the warm wear in your pack. The whole idea is to walk cool and rest warm.

Walking techniques

Your comfort is affected also by the way in which you walk. I doubt whether there is really any one style of walking which is best. Some people suggest ambling along with hands in pockets, conserving all energy that isn't involved in lifting your feet. Others suggest stepping out smartly, arms swinging to add momentum to your body, while you kick your feet forward at the end of every step to gain some extra ground over the day. You can try both methods and see which you find the less tiring. However, the following general considerations will probably be more helpful.

Keeping your back straight and your head up allows your lungs to work more efficiently and you become less breathless on the slopes. You can see more this way, too. At the same time, you must watch out for your feet. Given the fact that you need slip only once to break an ankle, it is of great importance to place the sole of your boot firm and flat on the ground.

For safety's sake you should stop completely when you wish to take one of those long gazes at the panorama all around you, or when you want to take a photograph, a compass bearing, or remove a piece of chocolate from its wrapper. As you walk, you should be searching the route ahead of you, noting the obstacles, choosing the easiest way through and, of course, looking out for items of interest.

Climbing the steeper slopes does require some special techniques. Your actual pace shouldn't alter, but as the gradient gets stiffer, so your step gets shorter, until there's barely a boot's length between your feet. Placing them flat and choosing your footing with care become even more important; if you slip now, you'll fall a long way. So will any stones or rocks you may dislodge, and even a small pebble can gather speed and debris very fast as it slides downhill. For this reason extra care is essential. If you do start something rolling, you should immediately stop and call out clearly 'Below!'

Coming downhill is in some ways even tricker, particularly with a heavy pack. Should you fall, the pack will pull you down on to your back in which position it's even more difficult to stop. You should bend slightly at the knees and waist, therefore, as though you're just about to sit down. It feels awkward at first but makes it much easier to keep your balance

Fig. 7   Stance when descending steep slopes: centre of gravity should be kept firmly over uphill foot.

and allows your legs to absorb the shock as you drop downwards. If the slope is very steep don't attempt to take it direct. You shouldn't really be attempting it at all, but if it is unavoidable traverse the slope in zig-zags, taking particular care when you turn the corner at the end of each leg. Novices tend to feel safer leaning backwards as they descend, but this rather encourages your legs to slip from under you. The secret is to lean forwards, keeping the weight firmly over the balls of your feet.

One further trick used by experienced mountaineers is well worth learning at the start: it is the 'rest step'. Once mastered, it gives tired muscles valuable respite on rough terrain. As your weight comes on to the forward foot straighten the leg and lock the knee backwards for a moment. All your weight is then taken by the linked bone structure of leg and pelvis, and not the muscle. Bend the knee again as you bring the back foot forward and repeat the procedure with the next step.

Hill hazards

Allowing the party to spread out can bring on a whole host of problems, so stick together. Your pace should be that of the slowest member. If you start off your walk slowly – at a mere stroll, even – the most natural speed for the group will soon establish itself. It's when you set off at a good speed that someone sooner or later finds that he can't keep it up and begins to fall behind. With larger parties a good rule is to walk in pairs and for the leaders to ensure that they can see the last two whenever they glance back. After any obstacle, such as a stile or a rock outcrop, the leaders should wait until everyone is across before continuing. It's a good idea, too, if as a leader you pause every now and then even in normal terrain to let the party re-form.

The least experienced members should be kept in the middle, with a particularly responsible person at the rear to ensure that no one begins to lag behind unnoticed, and to help along those who seem to need encouragement.

You'll find it less tiring if, having gained height at the

beginning of a walk, you try and maintain it. Plan your route with this in mind. Ridges or spurs radiating from a summit, however, often end in cliffs, the tips having been chopped off by glaciers some while ago. Remember this when following them down to low ground! Until you're well experienced, always try to descend the gentler slopes; it's not only safer but usually quicker in the end. Never run down hills or slide down snow slopes. Theoretically, this is safe enough if you can see the whole slope and there's a good smooth run-out at the bottom, but it's still too easy to lose control.

Following a stream downhill also has its dangers. Water will find the quickest route, which may include cliffs; or one bank may become impassable, involving a dangerous crossing. You'll find more on these matters on page 63.

We've already noted the virtues of Vibram-type boot soles, but in certain conditions they can be dangerous. They will not grip well on wet, mossy or greasy rock, or on hard snow and ice. One often hears warnings about them being slippery on wet grassy slopes, too, but I find that pressing one's feet down firmly does minimize this risk. Traditional nailed boots are supposed to work where Vibrams don't, but the rubber soles are so much better in so many other respects, including comfort, that nails needn't really be considered for general purpose walking boots. Beware of the limitations of Vibram soles, though; they aren't infallible.

We've noted also the importance of being weather-wise and if conditions do deteriorate badly, don't hesitate to turn back. It may be disappointing, but there will be another time when you can do the whole route, which there just might not be if you continue. At this stage the same caution applies to travelling at night. Remember that in winter, or even spring and autumn when the weather's dull, the days are short, and getting benighted is all too easy. If you do get caught out, and the end of your trek is not very near, it's best to seek shelter and wait until daylight; if possible letting your check-point know what you're doing.

Rest and shelter

Resting is an essential part of walking; some say that it's the best part. Being tired is no fun, so a pause every hour or so is quite in order. Don't stop for long or you'll spoil the rhythm you've set – and you'll begin to stiffen up if walking is still a new game to you. Take five minutes, though, to loosen boot laces and let the air get to your feet. Shed your pack and flex your shoulders, change sweat-damp socks for dry ones if you're on a long expedition with much walking ahead of you, and have a bite to eat. Such breaks also serve as focal points to which you can look forward on dull stretches of the route.

These five-minute stops are best made in a reasonably sheltered spot. The lee side of a rock or a wall are obvious places. A bunch of gorse can also break the wind. In winter conditions I have found a hollow in a snow-drift cosy, while a howling gale was blowing the spindrift horizontally two feet above my head. You shouldn't be out in such conditions yet, of course, and a simple dip in the ground may be all you require.

When it's raining – and also when the sun is particularly hot – to get beneath a roof for a few moments can be bliss. The roof may be the entrance of a cave, but resist the temptation to explore its depths – you're not equipped for it – or it may just be an overhanging rock. Derelict buildings, such as disused barns and old houses left from the days of subsistence farming, are really quite common if you look for them, and they're usually marked on the map but look out for notices warning of danger. If it hasn't been raining long enough for the water to percolate through the foliage, even a group of trees is better than nothing. Beware, though, of staying too long. Once the drips do start, they seem even wetter than rain.

Shelter for the lunch stop can be more carefully chosen, and more elaborate. An attractive site is a definite psychological asset, but more important is to find somewhere that isn't too cramped. You need somewhere to stretch out your legs, rest your back, place your stove or vacuum flask without upsetting it, and room for your pack to lie handy without being in the way. And it should be sheltered, wherein lies the problem.

Damp ground doesn't matter too much; you can sit on your sportsman's blanket or your waterproofs, but you really ought to get out of any rain and wind. If no natural shelter is available, many backpackers pitch the flysheet of their tent. For this reason you might consider carrying one if showers are expected, but again, given a sportsman's blanket or a bivvy sheet, you can soon improvise something (building shelter is something of an art – see page 133).

The reason for taking such care over choosing the lunch site is that you'll want to stay there for some little while. During that time, apart from eating and relaxing, you can discuss the day so far. Now is the moment to assess your activities and decide whether you're achieving what you set out to do. If there have been any problems, analyse them. Discuss also the prospects for the afternoon. Take a good look at the map and try to envisage once more what you'll be walking through in the light of what you've already seen. You cannot work too hard at developing your map craft. Bearing in mind that on your first few day-treks you are trying to learn the skills of the expeditioner you may find it useful at this point to make a few notes on the notepad you brought with you, just so that you can remember the details for the future.

Navigation

Getting lost is totally irresponsible. It will bear further emphasis that, at this stage of your hiking career, your route must be sufficiently well defined, both on the ground and on your map, so that if weather conditions suddenly deteriorate and visibility drops to a few yards you can still see your way along it.

Given such a route, navigation is largely a matter of keeping your eyes open and using a little common sense. The golden rule is to know exactly where you are on the map every yard of the way. On a 1:25,000 map there is so much detail that you should have no difficulty in identifying everything around you. On the 1:50,000 map your choice of features is a little less extensive, but still clear enough. Constant orientation, to give this process its proper name, is all you need to do 95 per cent of the time. Occasionally, though, you will find this too inaccurate, and you will need other techniques.

An instant check can be made by using *transits*. A transit is simply a line drawn between two landmarks. The procedure is to look around you and find two prominent features already in line. For example, a couple of farm houses further down the valley may appear to be one behind the other, or the corner of a field may line up with the edge of a plantation. It doesn't matter what you choose, as long as both items can be found on the map.

Draw a line – an imaginary one will do – between the two objects on the map and continue it onwards until it intersects your route. There is your position. You can double check with another transit so that the two lines intersect with a cross to mark the spot. If you've strayed from your route at all, you'll have to use two transits anyway to establish your position.

Sometimes, however, there are just no suitable transits, and in addition there's always some risk that you'll misidentify them on the map, particularly if they're not very obvious. In such cases your compass comes into play and you start taking bearings.

By pointing the direction of travel arrow at a really conspicuous feature which you can positively identify on the map, and turning the bezel of the compass so that the needle touches the north mark, you can read off the compass bearing. Adjust for variation and lay the compass on the map with the edge of the base plate passing through the feature at which you sited and the direction of travel arrow pointing towards the feature. Don't touch the bezel, but swing the whole compass until the north mark points northwards along the north/south grid lines on the map. Check that the edge of the base plate is still passing through the feature sighted. You are somewhere along the line represented by that edge. As with transits, you can repeat the procedure with another feature, to obtain *cross-bearings*. (*Resection* is another term often used.)

You can also use the compass to check the general direction in which you're heading. Just point the direction of travel arrow the way you're going, turn the bezel until the needle touches the north mark and compare your heading with what your route card says it should be. It is good practice to set your compass to the right heading at the start of each leg of the route. Then, by pointing the direction of travel arrow straight ahead of you and turning yourself until the needle touches the north mark, you can be sure that you're pointing in the right direction.

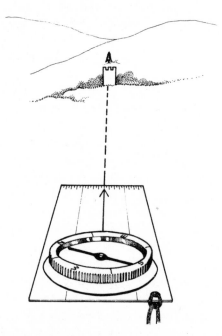

Fig. 8   Taking compass bearings: note also that tree and church tower are in transit; a line drawn through them on the map would give the same information as taking a bearing.

When you're following a footpath, of course, the exact compass heading is always changing – few footpaths are straight – but by a combination of these methods and careful reference to the map you can check the direction of every single bend. Do remember that it's the *red* end of the needle that points north; and do ensure, when you're working from map to terrain, that you have the direction of travel arrow pointing the right way. Failure to do either can result in your reading off the reciprocal of the bearing, which will put you 180° out. And in case you think you're never likely to do anything so foolish, let me admit that recently I did just that – for the first time that I can remember in over twenty years – in thick cloud on top of the Glyders in Snowdonia. If I hadn't spotted the mistake in time I'd have taken an involuntary 600m jump down into the Llanberis Pass!

You can gain invaluable help with developing your navigational skills by recording every check you make on the back of your blank route card. At the same time, you can fill in the card with the details of your actual route, as you progress. Of greatest importance here are the columns headed 'Time' and 'Terrain'. You can compare these with the original card and see how accurate you were at the planning stage. If the two disagree violently, find shelter, sit down and work out your route from scratch very carefully, because either you've miscalculated or you can't read a map – probably both.

Problems

Make absolutely no mistake; you have no right to be getting into trouble. Emergencies hit you only when you don't see them coming; so look, think, plan ahead. If you do get well and truly stuck, then stop, make yourself comfortable and wait. You will be rescued, although you may not deserve it! This section does not attempt to tell you how to handle a crisis: such information can be found throughout Chapter 8.

Nevertheless, there may be minor problems. The unforeseen does happen, despite all our attempts to sneak a preview. The two most common ones, apart from getting lost, are underestimating the length and difficulty of the route, and sudden deterioration of the weather. Your first reaction must be to stop, seek shelter and take stock of the situation. Minor problems, such as broken pack straps or slightly scraped knuckles, can easily be dealt with by recourse to your problem pack, and they make a good excuse to stop for a brew-up. If the problem is fatigue or weather, you must think more seriously.

Alterations in the planned route should never be undertaken lightly. The planning of more difficult treks should take into account possible escape routes back to civilization from several points along the main route, for use in the event of any major problem. Apart from these, anything you plan in the field and under stress will probably not be as well considered as the original. So, if you can stick to your pre-arranged route without risking your neck or giving your check-point a chance to raise the alarm, do so.

If the condition of the party or the weather looks like becoming so bad that your route just has to be altered – shortened, for instance, or at least made easier – you *must* first plan the revised version as carefully as the original; and it is *essential* that you arrange to reach civilization and inform your check-point *as soon as safely possible*.

When planning escape routes, it should be realized that the shortest way is seldom the quickest or the safest. It is much easier, for example, to follow a ridge to low ground, perhaps travelling on the lee side, just below the top, than it is to scramble down a steep slope straight into the valley. It is much less tiring to follow a footpath that takes you indirectly to your destination than it is to try and cross farm land with its obstacles of walls, barbed wire and livestock. Such an exercise would be against the spirit of the country code anyway. Crossing streams and rivers that can't easily be stepped over dry shod from boulder to boulder, or which are more than ankle-deep is, again, only for fools or experts.

In a serious emergency you might have to do all these things, but a serious emergency means that you're in trouble, and you shouldn't have got into trouble. When you're really experienced you may attempt such activities in the proper manner, but by then you will be skilled enough in route planning to avoid the necessity.

Practically all other minor problems can come under the heading of morale. You may get fed up with the purpose of your expedition, especially if it was rather contrived. You may fall out with your companions; or you may simply have had enough and feel demoralized by the distance yet to travel. Here is where resolution comes into play, but unless you actually enjoy being miserable, don't play too hard.

I have seen violent rows, fuelled by fatigue and ignited by a trivial mishap, such as someone's tea being knocked over, swiftly extinguished by the two characters concerned being ordered to laugh at each other. Consideration for your companions is, in fact, one of the keys to avoiding problems. It's worth cultivating what's called the 'buddy system', which means simply that you work at least in pairs, each one keeping an eye on the other to make sure that he doesn't overstep the limits of his ability. Making yourself responsible for the welfare of another, as well as yourself, is also one of the quickest ways I know of to develop your own skills.

If you put into practice all the advice given so far, you'll probably take problems in your stride without realizing that they've occurred, so make a point of being critical about everything that you do, and ask yourself, however successful a trip you've had, whether it could have been better. The only point here to beware of is taking it all over seriously. Don't get too intense about Doing the Right Thing. Remember: you're out in the open to enjoy yourself.

The return

In a way, treks always begin at the end. The satisfaction of having completed the course; of thinking, as you overhaul your gear, about how you might improve it; and about what you've seen and learnt, and what you're going to do next time, turn out to be the real purpose of the expedition.

The routine chores are obvious, but it's very tempting to leave them until the day after tomorrow, and when that happens, they have a habit of not getting done. Boots should be gently sponged clean with tepid water, their insides stuffed with newspaper or shoe-trees, and allowed to dry naturally away from artificial heat. If you try to dry them too quickly they can distort and even crack.

Shell clothing should be sponged clean, if necessary, and hung up to dry; then it should be put on a clothes hanger to prevent creasing and consequent damage to the waterproofing. Other personal gear should be cleaned and stowed safely, not left lying around to get lost, misused or damaged. Any repairs necessary – there shouldn't really be any if you're careful with your gear – should be put in hand immediately. And now it's time to write up the log.

Keeping a written account of expeditions can be a chore or it can be fun. Unfortunately most people seem to think they should write a vast screed about the details of the terrain, the route and their routine actions. There's no need: it's already on one or other of the route cards. The log can be more of a personal diary of your impressions and opinions, the details of which you will no doubt have written down on your notepad in the field anyway. A brief line about ground conditions and weather is in order, with further comment on how they affected you; and a list of any problems which occurred, with a note on how you might have avoided them, is most useful.

This log, written when your feet have stopped aching, and any other discomforts of the trail have mellowed in the light of the day's pleasures, will be your inspiration for the next time. And next time you'll probably want to go a few steps further and tackle more difficult terrain. The next chapter points the way.

4 Further Skills

Wild country

We've referred to wild country several times so far without really explaining what it is. A rough definition would be that wild country is any place where help, or a phone, and artificial shelter is more than an hour away. If you think about this, you'll realize that weather conditions have much to do with deciding if the country is wild or not. A route that's simple enough when it's fine can be bleak indeed when it's blowing and raining, or even dangerous when covered with ice or snow.

In practice, wild country in Britain can be thought of as occurring in the following areas: Dartmoor and Exmoor; the Brecon Beacons and the Black Mountains; the Mid and North Wales Mountains; the Peak District; the Isle of Man; the Pennines and the Cheviots; the Upper Yorkshire Dales; the Lake District; the North York Moors; the Sperin Mountains and the North Antrim Hills; the Galloway Hills; the Scottish Highlands; the Isles of Skye, Arran, Harris and Lewis. Some of these are so wild, they're downright savage. You shouldn't consider heading for them until you've practised all the skills in Chapter 3, and a few more. These new techniques often require the use of additional equipment, so we'll look at this gear next.

The walking rope

This is perhaps the most important piece of extra equipment for the beginner. Walking rope is thinner than the sort used for climbing; size No 2, which is 7mm in diameter, is the usual. Nylon is the best material because of its resilience – it can stretch 40 per cent before it breaks, and this helps to absorb the shock should you fall while tied to it. The most useful length is

about 36m. Since you're going to be carrying it as an
emergency measure, rather than as a standard tool, there's no
need to carry enough for every member of the group to rope up
at once, but with this much you can use it doubled which is
necessary in at least one application, and still have enough
length to be useful.

Fig. 9 Screw gate karabiner:
keep pin and screw lightly oiled.
Karabiners are made from high-
tensile strength alloy but can
crack if subjected to
compression shocks; take care
never to drop them.

A worthwhile additional investment, though by no means
essential, is a karabiner. Steel is cheaper but alloy is lighter.
Buy a big one – 11mm is ideal – and make sure it has a screw
gate for extra security. This item can be used as a pulley; it
makes belaying easier, and can be used for abseiling. You
might also consider carrying a sling which is a rope loop, about
2m being the most useful length.

You might think you now have the basis of a rock climber's
gear, but don't be tempted to use it for this purpose. As you'll
see from the next section, rope and accessories are purely to
provide extra safety in manoeuvres which might be frightening
but are in no way impossible without them. Don't use this gear
for taking short cuts, or for tackling routes which you wouldn't
contemplate otherwise: it's not designed for such uses, and it's
just not strong enough.

Rope handling

Rope is expensive and needs careful looking after. Try not to let it chafe on hard corners, though this might be difficult to avoid in the field; don't leave it kinked or coiled too tightly. Don't tread on it for you'll grind dirt into the heart. Wash it reguarly in tepid water and mild detergent and it should last you a long time.

To help prevent kinking when you break out a coiled rope, run the whole length through your hands first letting it form a neat pile at your feet. As long as you don't kick it about and as long as you lead the rope away from the top end it shouldn't tangle.

Coiling a rope is most easily done by sitting on the ground and winding it round under the soles of your boots and over your knees. Leave the last metre or so hanging free, and double the other end back on itself for about 30cm. Then wind the free-hanging end round the doubled-back portion and tuck the end through the protruding loop and pull both ends tight. The whole coil is now securely held; neither end can come unravelled, but it can be broken out easily. Figure 10 illustrates this, along with some of the more useful knots which should provide you with all you need. Practise these knots until you can tie them in the dark with gloves on. It's not impossible that one day, in an emergency, you might have to do just that!

Basic rope techniques

Before learning how to use the rope there are a few simple technical terms you need to know. To *belay* means to tie yourself securely to a strong point, or *anchorage*, such as a tree trunk, rock spike or even a complete boulder. The *active part* of the rope is the bit that will take any strain between you and the next person should he slip. The *inactive part* is obviously the bit that isn't doing anything. *Tying on* means fixing the rope to yourself, whether or not you're belayed.

To tie yourself on to the end of a rope, take one end and pass a couple of turns round your waist. At the front tie a bowline

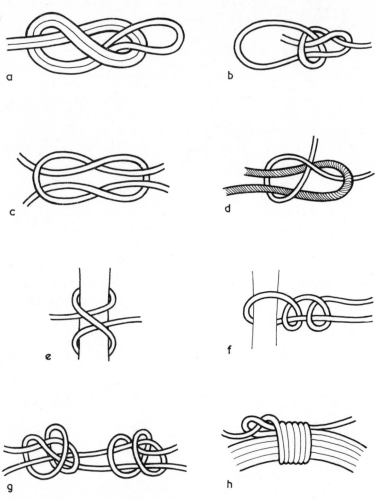

Fig. 10 Knots: (a) *Figure of eight* loop in doubled end of rope; (b) *bowline* for making a loop in a rope end; (c) *reef knot* for joining two rope ends of equal thickness; (d) *sheet bend* for joining two ropes of unequal thickness (the shaded rope is the thicker); (e) *clove hitch* used in lashings; (f) *two half hitches* useful for securing a rope end; (g) *double fisherman's bend* used for making rope slings; (h) method of securing a coiled rope.

close up to your stomach, and with the free end tie two half-hitches round the loops on your waist. The point is that should you slip and the rope come taut the loops round your waist will not so easily be pulled tight and cut you in half.

The traditional way of using a walking rope is for the

members of the group to tie themselves on at equal points along the line. The idea is that if one member should slip the others can hold him. In practice, you would tend to rope up on difficult terrain – a steep icy slope, for example – where no one's footing is going to be that secure. The sudden jerk of a falling companion can be enough to pull you off your own balance, and the whole party falls, which is not quite the idea. It is slower, but far safer, when you're roped up, to move one at a time while the rest of the group remains belayed. This works best with no more than two people on the rope, and four is the maximum number. It's worth remembering that No 2 walking line isn't really strong enough to hold more than one person in a fall.

The simplest belay is where the rope leads from your waist round an anchorage behind you. You then take a loop of the active part where it leads back past you and tie it with two half-

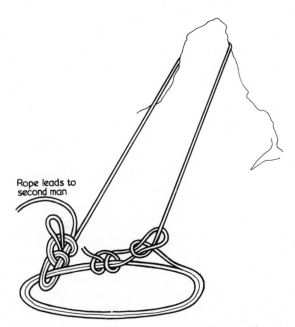

Rope leads to
second man

Fig. 11   Tying on and belaying: anchorage should be well above waist height if there is any chance of belay slipping off under load. Knots are best positioned at back.

hitches into the loops around your waist. A variation useful where it's difficult or inconvenient to pass the main rope round the belay point, is to thread your sling behind it, clip the ends together with your karabiner and pass the rope through that, before tying back the active part as above. As a hill walker you shouldn't have need of any more sophisticated method of belaying. Do beware of getting into the situation where you've inadvertently become a rock climber!

Once you are safely belayed the other person can move. As he goes he flicks the rope running out after him behind any little flake or lump of rock that's handy. Should he fall, he'll go no further than the distance between him and that last *running belay* as it's called. You, meanwhile, have to pay the rope out, or take it in as appropriate, so that it remains just taut between you. It's done as follows.

Hold the rope so that it runs across your back close in to your waist. Grasp the active part at the point where it leaves your body and take a single twist of the other, inactive, end of the rope round the wrist of your other hand. This hand holds the rope at arm's length low in front of you, keeping the line into your hip. To pay out, pull your inactive hand into your hip and stretch your active arm out, pulling the rope across your back. Next, slide your inactive hand out again and bring your active hand into your waist. Repeat the process to continue paying out. Taking in is just the reverse. Move only one hand at a time, keeping a firm hold on the rope with the other.

As soon as your companion reaches a safe stance, with a good anchorage to hand, he belays and brings you to him, your roles being reversed. Obviously, the better man goes first when you're ascending a slope but, less obviously, he comes last when you're descending, so that he's always above and ready to hold you should you fall.

There's a standard system of signals for use when you're roped up; if you learn them and stick to them, there will be no confusion. When the leader has belayed, he calls out, 'Taking in', and when he's taken in all the slack the second man calls out, 'That's me'. The leader then prepares himself and calls out, 'Climb when ready'. The second replies, 'Climbing', waits

Fig. 12   Tending the rope: ensure that feet are firmly placed and that rope from waist to anchorage is kept taut. Flake spare rope down carefully.

for the leader to shout, 'Aye aye', and starts off. Should he feel that the rope's too slack while he's climbing, he calls, 'Take in'. If it's too tight, he calls, 'More slack'. It seems pedantic, but, not being a rock climber, your margin of safety in situations that make a rope advisable is so slight that you just have to get things right.

It will bear repeating that having a walking rope with you, and having learnt these few skills, does not justify you indulging in technical rock climbing. But, if you're at all unhappy with conditions, you rope up; and to hell with all those who go steaming past, eyebrows raised.

Fig. 13 Classic abseil: pointing lower foot down hill helps to ensure correct stance.

Abseiling

Another rope technique which belongs to the climbers, but which you might consider using with caution on steep slopes, is abseiling. This is a method of sliding down a rope which is doubled round a belay point so that both halves hang down the face. Once you're at the bottom you can then pull gently on one end of the rope and bring the whole lot down to you. We'll consider only one method: the *classic*.

It is done as follows. Stand with your back to the slope, between the slope and the belay point, and with your feet astride the double rope. Pick it up behind you with your right hand so that it passes between your legs, pass it up across your chest, over your left shoulder and down across your back to a point about a foot behind your right hip. Hold it there with your right hand. Place your left hand on that part of the rope which now leads from you to the belay point, and grasp it just firmly enough to steady yourself, Now walk *slowly* backwards down the face, keeping your legs as much at right angles to it as possible. You'll find that you can adjust your speed by the exact angle at which you hold the rope with your right hand. Don't hold the rope in your left hand too tightly; just lean back on the line around your right thigh and left shoulder, letting these areas take the strain. Keep the right leg lower than the left and the rope well up under the buttock.

With this method, you run the risk of burning more than your hands, so *go slowly!* On long, steep pitches it can be painful, but it's ideal for the odd 5m drop down which you want to make a carefully controlled descent.

The ice-axe

Unless you confine your expeditioning to the four months or so of our British summer, you'll sooner or later find yourself walking on snow. In the Scottish Highlands, indeed, you can find snow all year round; and of course if you ever get as far as the Alps . . .

On snow, in wild country, you need an ice-axe. This tool consists of a steel head, which looks like a small pick-axe. One end, the *pick*, is usually curved and saw-toothed to provide good grip when driven into hard snow or ice. The other end, or *adze*, is shorter and flattened out to a broad chisel edge. This is useful for hacking out steps on steep snow slopes, digging snow holes or clearing footholds of ice.

Most axes have a hole in the centre of the head through which a karabiner can be clipped, or through which a short sling can be threaded. The idea of the sling is that you can wind it round your wrist as a safety line in case you should drop the axe. Holding on to the axe at all times becomes instinctive with experience, but novices certainly are advised to use a sling.

The handle, or *shaft*, of the axe can be made of laminated wood, steel or fibreglass, and ends in a *ferrule*, or steel spike at the bottom. This grips well when you use the tool as an extra leg on icy ground. All three points of the axe are sharp and potentially lethal, so keep them covered when not in use with the special rubber protectors you can buy.

Fig. 14 Ice axe: most axes are supplied with slings. Ensure that one is fitted in the shop.

Ice-axes come in various lengths and should be selected for the exact sort of job they're required for. For walking, choose one that reaches from the ground to the point where your hand joins your wrist. This is slightly longer than is usually recommended, but allows you to use the axe as a walking stick on level ground. Using the axe as a walking stick is not usually recommended either; it's supposed to blunt the ferrule. Maybe it does, but it makes a lot more sense than the all-too-common sight of hill walkers scrabbling about on icy paths, with short axes strapped to their rucksacks.

Prices vary widely, too. For walking, you don't need an expensive axe. Something like the Chouinard Bernina, or the MSR Thunderbird is ideal.

Apart from using it as a walking stick, the axe, just like the walking rope, should be carried as a safety precaution. Don't head deliberately into situations where its use is essential. On the other hand, don't hesitate to use it anywhere that it helps. If you're cutting steps in snow make them good and deep, so that you can get your whole foot in, and stagger them left and right to minimize the chance of their collapsing into each other when your weight comes on them. On very steep slopes you can hold the axe head in your uphill hand, thumb under the adze, palm over the top, and pick pointing to the ground. As you ascend, drive the pick into the snow at shoulder height to give you a hand hold. On narrow paths near steep ground, or when you're traversing a slope, hold the axe like a walking stick, again in the uphill hand, and drive the ferrule deep into the snow beside you for support. The pick should be pointing backwards, as this puts it in the right position for using the axe as a brake should you fall.

This use of the axe as a brake is its most important function. If you're holding the axe as described above, getting it into the right position is a quick, almost automatic, movement. The head comes up level with your shoulder, pick pointing to the snow. The shaft slopes down to the opposite side and is grasped about two-thirds of the way down with your other hand. When you fall, roll on to your front and press the pick into the snow, using your elbow as a fulcrum. Don't jab too hard or the axe will be snatched from your grasp, but press steadily as you slide.

Fig. 15   Fall arrest: here, right arm guides axe head which is brought in to left shoulder. Feet are kept well clear of snow.

You'll find this easier if you keep the axe in to your shoulder rather than at arm's length. If you're falling head first, you must pivot on the axe head until your feet are pointing downhill before pressing down fully. The danger here is that you will over-run the axe and impale yourself on it. Once the pick starts to bite, lift the ferrule clear of the snow. If it digs in, it will lift the pick out of the snow and you'll sommersault out of control.

Obviously, when you're flying down a slope towards a 30m cliff, with the snow flaying the skin off your face and your heart wrapped round your tonsils, you're not really going to have the presence of mind to *think* about how to do a fall-arrest. You simply *must* practise it on safe, gentle slopes until it becomes instinctive. Even better, avoid climbing about on steep snow slopes above 30m cliffs.

Crampons

One final item of special equipment is a pair of crampons. These, too, are intended for snow conditions, and consist of spiked steel soles which strap on to your boots to provide a better grip – that is when you aren't freezing your fingers off trying to adjust the straps, or catching the spikes in your gaiters.

For the serious mountaineer they are a necessity, but for the hill walker to carry them on the off-chance that he might need them as a safety aid doesn't seem very realistic. If conditions are such that your ice-axe alone doesn't provide adequate protection, you can improve the odds against you by putting your spare socks on over your boots. They'd better be woollen, though; nylon is even more slippery than vibram soles! If the whole of your route is covered with hard snow or ice leave it to the climbers until you've had some practical instruction.

Difficult terrain

Even when you don't need to use the gear discussed above there are some further skills you'll need for wild country.

To continue with the snow theme, you'll find it much easier

in deep snow if you play follow-my-leader and step exactly in the prints of the person in front. Change the lead regularly to give the front man a rest from making tracks. Watch also that snow doesn't ball up on your boots as this makes them grip even less, and is in any case most uncomfortable.

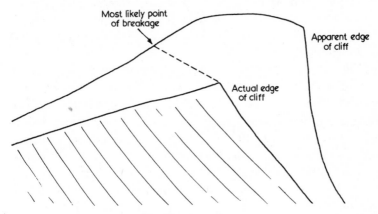

Fig. 16   A cornice.

When there's plenty of snow, then, along ridges, in the tops of gullies, or at the edge of escarpments, you'll almost certainly find cornices. These are lips of overhanging snow – a sort of drift hanging in mid-air above the drop. They're likely to break off without warning so move carefully if you have to traverse one, and keep well away from the edge. Figure 16 shows that they tend to break much further down the slope than you'd think. If you're at all inexperienced both rope and ice-axe should be used here.

Avalanches may seem improbable in this country but every year people are killed by them. They usually occur when the snow is thawing, or after a fresh fall on top of old hard snow. In addition a feature known as *windslab* where a cold wind has frozen a hard crust on to the top of soft snow can produce a seemingly firm surface which is in fact treacherously poised ready to slide. If you do get caught in an avalanche then, theoretically, you get rid of your pack and ice-axe – fast – and swim against it, using a sort of back stroke. In practice, you'll find praying almost as effective!

One tends to forget that snow, like rain, will make you wet. You really do need gaiters and overtrousers. You'll almost certainly be wearing your cagoule against a chill wind but if there's any snow falling, put your hood up. It sounds obvious, but I've seen many people walking around with soggy balaclavas! And finally, at the risk of sounding a kill-joy, chucking snowballs isn't very sensible. Think about getting one down your neck and you'll realize why.

The following technique certainly does not apply in snow conditions; if there's any about, don't try it. Scree-running is a quick way of losing height. It's exciting – and dangerous. The trick is to find a smooth, long scree slope of small loose stones. Lean forward, with the weight squarely on the balls of your feet, bend a little at the knees and waist, and walk straight down, taking small steps and digging your heels in. It's called 'running' because in practice that's precisely what you'll find yourself doing.

Stop every now and then by side stepping, turning your feet to run across the scree as you do so, as each step you take starts a minor avalanche which will soon go out of control if you don't give the scree frequent opportunities to stop moving. For the same reason, don't move directly one behind the other, and don't space yourselves too far apart; a close arrowhead formation is reckoned to be the best. Keeping your arms loosely splayed out helps your balance. The sensation is rather like flying – but it plays havoc with your boots.

Next comes scrambling, about which I have mixed feelings. The line between scrambling, which is making your way up slopes where you have to use your hands as well as feet, and proper climbing, which needs ropes and expert tuition, is very difficult to draw. If you do have to scramble, remember the following points. First, look for the easiest route up; second, try and plan your hand and foot holds before you start. Keep hand holds low where possible – between waist and shoulder height – and keep each step as short as you can. Stand upright away from the rock, keeping your heels down so that your boot soles are horizontal. On a long scramble look for a good stance on which to rest every 20m or so, but otherwise don't hang about. Clinging on to a finger-wide crack, while your big toe balances on 2cm-wide ledge will soon have your muscles quaking. It's also the point at which scrambling becomes climbing.

For river-fording, and by this is meant anything that involves your going into the water more than ankle-deep, you must rope up. One person belays to an anchorage on the bank, upstream of the point where you've decided to cross. The person crossing ties on to the rope and moves down to the crossing place, while his belayed partner pays out the rope. He then loosens his rucksack straps and casts off his waist belt so that he can shed the pack easily should he fall, and makes his way across, facing the flow of water and shuffling sideways, working his way downstream diagonally. Should he fall, he will automatically swing back to the bank without travelling far. Once across, he belays to a point on the bank, up-stream of the crossing place, and brings his companion to him. With more than two people involved, the second man casts off the rope, once he's across, and the first man recovers it, before repeating the procedure with the third.

If possible strip off all your lower clothing, particularly your socks. Keeping this gear dry is worth any trouble you can take. Wear your boots, however, and try to dry them off as much as possible, along with the rest of you, when you reach the other side. In very deep water, arrange some buoyancy – empty water bottles, Karrimat, inflated polythene bags, anything you can press into service. Use a long stick to sound the depth.

The best advice of all, however, for any river-fording is simple. *Don't.* Try to remember that mountain streams can change their character very quickly. A gentle rivulet that you jump across on your way out in the morning can become a rushing spate following rainfall, that poses quite a problem on your return in the evening. There are few rivers, or even streams, in this country that aren't spanned fairly frequently by bridges of some sort. Plan your route to cross at these points. If you do have to ford a river, it's a sign either of poor map craft at the planning stage of your trek, or that you're lost.

Wayfinding

As we saw earlier, you've no excuse for getting lost but in wild country finding the way can be tricky. When you reach the stage of heading out across pathless terrain, you'll need to use as many aids to navigation as you can in addition to your map and compass. We've already discussed transits and cross-bearings; here now are a few more subtle variations.

When walking along a pre-set compass bearing, it's best to sight your compass at an object straight ahead on that bearing and then walk to it before repeating the procedure. The object may be a hilltop 5km away, or a tussock of grass 5m away. The further off the better it is, but the important thing is not to bury your nose in the compass dial while you're walking or you won't see where you're going.

A useful trick, to check that the direction in which you've been travelling from a prominent landmark is the one you started out on when you left it, is to sight along the compass back towards the landmark. The *white*, south-seeking end of the needle should touch the north mark without your moving the bezel. If it doesn't, you've wandered off course. This is known as a *back bearing*. If the reason why this works isn't obvious to you, go back and look again at the section on navigation in Chapter 3.

Whilst on the subject of compasses, remember that the scales marked on the base plate can be useful. Depending on the scale of your map, you can work out how many divisions of the base plate scale represent 100m on the ground. Using these divisions, you can measure distances very accurately.

When using the compass in the dark, it's not much use relying on any luminous markings that it may have on it. Night-time navigation needs to be meticulous and the luminous markings by themselves simply don't allow sufficient accuracy. Peering at a compass by torch light does tend to spoil your night vision but the cure is simple, and applies to all use of the torch at night: shut one eye. When you switch the torch off and open the eye again, you'll find its night vision unimpaired. You can see in the dark with one eye at least!

The sort of torch you carry on expedition will give only about two hours useful light per battery. But if you use it sparingly, just flashing it on the ground ahead for a moment and memorizing the details of the next 5m, one battery can last all night. Don't try coming down steep rocky gullies this way, though! Give your night vision a chance, all the same, terrain permitting; it's amazing how good it can become once your eyes are used to the dark.

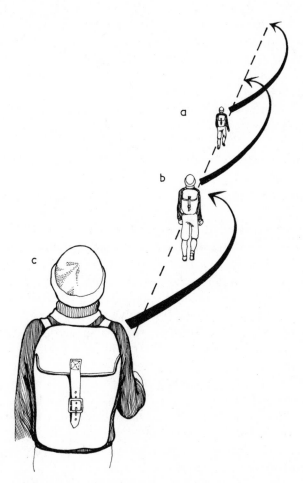

Fig. 17   Mobile transits: first two men (a and b) leapfrog past each other; the third (c) brings up rear, checking direction with compass and torch.

Transits are perfectly possible to find at night, though your choice of features will be limited mainly to what you can see against the skyline, and you must take great care to identify them correctly. Safer, probably, is the following system, well known to army personnel on night exercises. Send one person on ahead with a torch along the chosen compass bearing. About a hundred paces is a practicable maximum. He then turns and faces the rest of you, shining his torch straight at you. Check with your compass that he's on the correct bearing and if he's too far to one side, signal him to move over. It's important to get him exactly in position as any error here will be multiplied greatly over the next few minutes.

Now comes the ingenious bit. Send the next man in the group ahead with his torch. He goes beyond the first man by an equal distance, then turns and shines his torch at the first man. If you can see his torch and he can see yours he's off station. Signal him which way to move and then wait until his torch light disappears behind the first man. Now you can walk up to the first man and send him on ahead of the second to repeat the process. Once set up it's a fast way of travelling in straight lines at night.

The same trick can be used without the torches in day time when the terrain is particularly featureless, or when it's foggy. In the latter case, the second man moves only to the limit of visibility, keeping a frequent watch over his shoulder to make sure he doesn't go too far. Signals are made by waving your arms or your torch. This is preferable to shouting instructions which will often be misunderstood owing to your voice being distorted by echoes, the wind and so on.

Natural features can be used for purposes other than transits. A field wall, fence or stream, for example, if marked on the map, can be used as a *guideline*. This is as simple as walking along a footpath. You find one that's going in your direction and follow it; but check with your compass frequently to make sure that it is taking you where you want to go. You can use a contour line in the same way but this is rather more difficult. You have first to establish your position on the line, by taking cross-bearings for example, and then walk on, taking care not to gain or lose any height. This is called *contouring*. The tendency to beware of is to lose height and then over-compensate.

You can walk across open ground quite confidently if you know that you're going to be *collected* by some long natural feature – the wall or stream again – which crosses your track ahead. If you're trying to reach a particular point somewhere along this feature, the problem arises that you may be collected a little to one side of it. You then have to decide which way to turn to reach your objective, and it's easy to go the wrong way. To solve this one, *aim off* to one side of the point. For example, make slightly to the west of your objective, so that when you reach the collecting feature you know that you must turn to the east. It adds a little to the distance, but saves time and energy in the long run. Orienteerers, who have to navigate fast and accurately over difficult terrain in competition with each other, use this trick extensively.

They also learn to count their paces and to visualize distances on the map in terms of these units. This is perhaps going a little far for the average expeditioner, but it's useful to know your usual speed. Filling in your route card in the field, as explained under Navigation in Chapter 3, will give you the time and distance of each leg, so you can calculate your speed. Try and formulate average speeds over various types of terrain, during the course of several expeditions. In the event of your getting lost, you'll have one more piece of information with which to establish your position.

In conclusion, we ought briefly to mention navigation without a compass. It's not on. Theoretically, you can point the hour hand of your watch at the sun and, if the watch is accurate and reading Greenwich Mean Time, half-way between that and twelve o'clock is true south. At night you can look among the stars for the constellation of the Plough. It's the one that looks like a saucepan with a bent handle. Follow the front lip of the pan upwards and the first star you come to is Polaris, indicating true north. Unfortunately it's rather insignificant and easily missed. In any case, what happens when it's cloudy? All in all, you'd be better off ensuring that more than one person in the group has a compass. Then it doesn't matter even if you do drop one over a cliff!

Lost

Of course, you're not going to get lost, but, however good your navigation, there will be times when you're just not quite sure where you are. Actually, this isn't a joke. It's when you get into this situation and press on in the hope that you'll recognize something sooner or later, that you do get lost.

Assuming that you don't know where you are and you can't readily identify any of the features around you, stop, find shelter, sit down and think. Next, pinpoint on the map the last spot where you really did know where you were and work out how long you've been walking since. Knowing your average speed and the direction in which you've been travelling, you can now make a well-educated guess as to where you are on the map. Does the surrounding terrain fit?

If it does, then your problems are solved and all you have to do is to find your way back on to your route. If not, then don't panic. Look again on the map at the spot where you 'knew' where you were. You may have been wrong, so look back a little further and repeat the procedure. If this doesn't work, there are various other possibilities.

The most obvious is to try retracing your steps. If you've been observant as you travelled you'll recognize the details as you pass them on your way back. Carry on backtracking until you're absolutely sure you know where you are.

Alternatively, you can set about getting back to low ground, bearing in mind the reservations expressed in the section on hill hazards in Chapter 3. Aim for a really conspicuous collecting feature, the ideal one, of course, being a road. As long as you're not alone, which of course you shouldn't be, you can then thumb a lift to a phone and let your check-point know what's been happening.

The third possibility should be treated with caution. You can make for some local prominence – a hilltop or ridge – from which you may get a better all-round view and thereby be able to spot some feature that you can identify on the map.

Finally, depending on the weather and the condition of the party, you can admit that you're stuck and bivvy down to wait until the weather clears or you're rested, or – in extreme cases – until you're found. Don't make a habit of this last one; and do look at page 133–5.

Signalling

The only signals you will really need, for emergencies only, are the International Alpine Distress Signal of six blasts of a whistle, flashes of a torch or waves of a flag at ten-second intervals every alternate minute (see page 18) and possibly, two ground-to-air signals for use with helicopters (see pages 89 and 138).

However, for communicating between members of your group, either for fun or in situations such as when you're using each other as mobile transits, the Morse Code can be very useful. It's written out in full below. Column one contains the dots and dashes, more usually referred to as *dits* and *dahs*. In column two is the standard phonetic alphabet, giving you the letters which each of the Morse symbols represents. This is useful to remember, even if only for spelling out your name over the phone. Next to it, in column three, is another alphabet. If you say the words out loud you'll find that the italicized symbols, which carry the natural stress when spoken, correspond approximately to the dahs, and the unstressed syllables to the dits, of the Morse symbol. If you have a reasonably musical ear, you'll find this alphabet of great help in learning the code.

The Morse Code

. —	Alpha	A-*hoy*
— . . .	Bravo	*Bar*-ba-rous-ly
— . — .	Charlie	*Cal*-cu-*la*-tion
— . .	Delta	*Dan*-ger-ous
.	Echo	End
. . — .	Foxtrot	Fly-ing *Dutch*-man
— — .	Golf	*Game Keep*-er
. . . .	Hotel	Ho-ri-zon-tal

· ·	Item	Is-n't
· — — —	Juliet	Ju-*ly blue sky*
— · —	Kilo	*Kil*-ler *whale*
· — · ·	Lima	Lo-*gis*-ti-cal
— — ·	Mike	*M*oon *shine*
— ·	November	*Nan*-cy
— — —	Oscar	*Or-lan-do*
· — — ·	Papa	Po-*lice Pan*-da
— — · —	Quebec	*Queen Guin*-ev-*ere*
· — ·	Romeo	Ras-*pu*-tin
· · ·	Sierra	Sum-ma-ry
—	Tango	*T*ea
· · —	Uniform	Un-der-*neath*
· · · —	Victor	Vic-to-ry *roll*
· — —	Whiskey	With-*out doubt*
— · · —	X-ray	*X*-ray ma-*chine*
— · — —	Yankee	*Yel*-low *Rolls-Royce*
— — · ·	Zulu	*Z*o-*ol*-og-y

In sending Morse, the dit should last for one unit of time, the dah for three, and there should be a one-unit gap between each. The space between letters should be three units. They can be flashed by torch, even in day-time, if the weather's dull and you hold the torch against a dark background such as a rock. You can also send with a flag. Although it's not the conventional way, the following method is the best for our purposes. The dit is made by flicking it vertically over your head and the dah by waving it above you in a single figure of eight.

A suitable sending procedure is to attract the receiver's attention by sending V E (dit-dit-dit-dah dit). The receiver then sends K (dah-dit-dah) which means that he's ready to receive, or Q (dah-dah-dit-dah) which means Wait, and will be followed by K when he is ready. You can then start sending your message, but after each word you wait for the receiver to send T (dah) acknowledging that he's understood. If he doesn't send T, repeat the word until he does. At the end of your message, you send A R (dit-dah dit-dah-dit) and the receiver acknowledges with R (dit-dah-dit). A full stop is A A A (dit-dah dit-dah dit-dah) and to cancel what you've sent, use a succession of E's. This is admittedly a simplification of the standard procedure, but will suffice for private communication between yourselves. Sticking to it, and taking particular care with the timing, will make your signalling much easier to follow.

One word of warning, however: don't go flashing Morse around indiscriminately. Anyone else who sees it may very well mistake it for a distress signal. The same thing applies with torches, stoves and fires when you're in camp.

5 Camping Gear

The good and the bad

Just after I left school, I walked and hitch-hiked some 28,000km around continental Europe, Scandinavia, the Balkans and the Middle East, re-visiting in one grand tour places I'd been to in previous years – as well as many new ones! I carried an old A-frame rucksack, a calico tent from Millets and a kapok-filled, simple quilted sleeping-bag. So it can be done, with even the most primitive gear. But it was summer time, and I was lucky.

There were some hair-raising moments, nevertheless. I spent one night in the mountains of Anatolia with my feet wrapped round one tent pole, my arms round the other and my face buried in a shirt, desperately praying that I and my tent would survive the dust storm that raged for another seven hours. I survived, but the tent required a certain amount of work with needle and thread, and was never really the same again.

On another occasion, near the Arctic Circle, I sat huddled in my sleeping-bag, in the 2am twilight, with a nylon mesh shopper over my head, chain-smoking cigarettes (not easy inside a nylon mesh shopper) while the mosquitoes enjoyed the bloodiest jamboree of their parasitic lives. I can still hear the vicious whine of their wings as they zoomed gleefully in to the attack. In the morning I looked like a leper.

I spent as much time savagely kicking my unwieldy pack into some form of submission as I did in carrying the beast, and frequently I resorted to leaving it in left-luggage offices at local stations while I went off on blissfully lightweight three-day jaunts, with everything I really needed packed in that nylon shopper. Since then I have come to appreciate the value of good equipment.

A couple of years later I spent several comfortable nights by the side of a cleg infested tarn deep in the French Massif, while the horse-flies buzzed impotently outside the insect screen of the tent I'd borrowed. Later that year in the Jura Mountains I slept, stripped to the skin and perspiring richly in a down sleeping-bag, while the temperature outside it dropped below freezing. Admittedly, it was a very expensive bag – and it wasn't mine.

When it comes to major expeditioning there's simply no substitute for a first-class rucksack, sleeping-bag and tent. Whatever else you do without, these three items are worth going bankrupt for.

Packs

Since the pack is the thing you actually have to carry all the gear in it's worth buying this first and planning the rest of your gear to fit whichever type you find most comfortable; an unconventional method, no doubt, but I discovered it the hard way.

Whatever type of pack you buy, the design should allow most of the weight to be taken on your hips, which are the parts of your anatomy best able to cope with the extra load. This is usually achieved with a hip belt, a torso hugging back panel and a tall shape, narrow from front to back, to keep the centre of gravity as near your spine as possible. The dumpy old A-frame sacks merely invite back trouble.

Most modern sacks are made from PU coated nylon which is lighter than canvas, more rot resistant and more waterproof – at least when new. Don't dismiss canvas, though. It's more resistant to abrasion and can easily be waterproofed with a silicon spray, whereas nylon, when the PU coating wears off, needs to be painted with something like Evostick or clear Bostik. It works well enough but it's a messy business!

The traditional backpacking load carrier is the pack frame. Basically, this is a rectangular construction of strong, light alloy shaped to follow the curve of your back and looking not unlike a ladder. The rungs are curved to stand away from your back and wide webbing straps are stretched between the uprights. This arrangement spreads the load over your torso but allows an air space between you and the pack for ventilation. Good frames come with wide, padded hip belts and fully adjustable padded shoulder straps.

Take care with getting the right fit. With the belt around your hips – not your waist – the lower webbing strap should make contact just below the small of your back and the upper one with your shoulder blades. They don't have to be chosen for size as exactly as boots or jackets; they are sufficiently adjustable to suit a variety of backs, but individual models do differ in size and shape so you'll probably have to try several makes to find one which suits you. In terms of quality, names like Berghaus, Camp Trails and Karrimor are the ones to look for.

Cheap pack frames, usually sold complete with sack, are too often a liability. The frames are soft and bend easily; the sacks are flimsy, poorly made and non-waterproof, and being merely copies of the more expensive designs they tend not to get the details quite right; side pockets are too small to be useful, lids don't fit properly and fastening points for drawcords are ineffectively positioned. You'll see them advertised in the press occasionally, but, although they seem to be bargains, it's worth spending twice as much on a pack that will last five times as long.

Good frames are expensive, and you'll find the sack comes as an extra. To begin with, if you can't afford both, you can pack your gear into an army surplus kitbag and lash it to the frame with small cord. You can even use three or four dustbin liners. Some backpackers, indeed, prefer such a system. They do go for proofed nylon stuff bags rather than bin liners but the principle is the same and does allow you to unpack the one bag you need at any given time without disturbing the contents of the others.

A more recent development is the anatomic sack. I am now using one and find it just as good a load carrier while being rather more versatile. It can be hauled up cliffs like a frameless sack, stowed in luggage compartments or car boots more conveniently than the cumbersome pack frame, and, to my own mind, it fits the back more comfortably. It features an adjustable internal frame and a shaped and padded back panel designed to allow for ventilation while conforming to the wearer's shape exactly. The best of these are manufactured by Berghaus who produce the Cyclops range, and Karrimor who have introduced the Jaguar in several versions.

In both pack frame and anatomic sack, the accommodation is similar. There are usually two main compartments with the

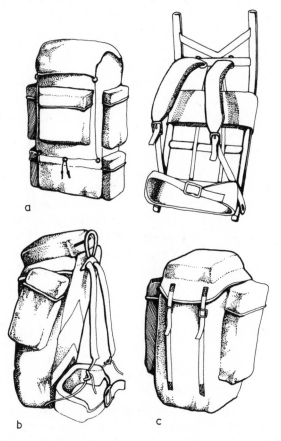

Fig. 18   Packs: (a) Camp Trails Ponderosa sack with Astral frame; (b) Karrimor Jaguar anatomic sack: (c) frameless rucksack.

lower one accessible through a zip in the front. The platform between the two has holes in the corners so that tent poles or other long items can be stowed upright using the full height of the pack. There are two to four sizeable side pockets and another big one on the lid. In the anatomic sack the top compartment can be extended with a light nylon sleeve which turns it into a true high loader, like the pack frame sack, and in some designs even allows it to be used as a bivvy bag if you empty out the contents.

A cheaper alternative to either of these packs is the frameless rucksack. A frameless pack naturally lacks the rigidity of its bigger brothers and is often rather more primitive in other respects; shoulder straps, for example, are capable only of limited adjustment and hip belts are not fitted, which means that they tend to hang from the shoulders rather than sit on the hips. These considerations add up to the fact that frameless packs are most suitable for packing the lighter loads on short, one or two night, trips. Think of 10–12kg as the maximum comfortable weight.

Having said this, it can be pointed out that, at least when you're new to the game, 10kg is ideally the maximum you should be carrying. A frameless pack, too, has all the versatility of an anatomic sack; and being less rigidly structured it will accommodate itself better to the backs of growing young people. The Outward Bound Mark I and II by Karrimor are well proven models while sacks like the Berghaus Monro and Adda, with padded back panels and provision for a hip belt, are excellent load carriers.

Sleeping-bags

The purpose of a sleeping-bag is quite simple. It surrounds you with a layer of still air which your body heat then warms up. At the same time it allows the $\frac{1}{2}$ litre or so of moisture you perspire every night to disperse into the atmosphere. Finally, so that you can carry it easily, it packs up to a small, lightweight bundle.

Because of its light weight and its ability to compress to practically nothing and then loft well time after time, bird down makes the most efficient filling. Unfortunately it has two great disadvantages: if it gets wet it collapses into a soggy, sorry-looking pulp which takes days to dry out; and it's very expensive. Mixtures of down and feather, as used in bags like Black's Icelandic range, are a little cheaper. They're not as warm as pure down but are usually adequate in temperatures down to freezing, provided that you dress warmly and use ground insulation – of which more later.

Fortunately, there are alternatives. Dacron Holofil and P3 are synthetic fibres developed specially as substitutes for down and many manufacturers are now using them. Fillings like these are heavier and bulkier than down for the same degree of insulation but they do still work when wet, and they're a lot less expensive. Beware, though, of the cheap terylene wadding used in mass-market bags. It's good enough for the tourist camp site or the caravan in summer, but that's about it.

As far as design and construction are concerned, avoid bags which are made from a single layer of quilting. Where the stitching lines come there's obviously no filling between you and the outside world so cold spots develop. A double layer of quilting, or box wall construction, in which the inner and outer shells of the bag are separated by baffles of thin material, provides a more even layer of insulation. Slant wall and overlap tube construction are more sophisticated variations on the same theme and are even more effective.

A tapered bag with its foot narrower than the head is warmer and lighter than a simple rectangle, and one with an oval shaped opening which can be pulled up into a hood so that only your nose and eyes peek out is even better. Another feature worth looking for is a boxed foot, in which the toe of the bag is shaped to retain its layer of filling even with your feet pressed up against it.

A versatile general purpose bag is the synthetically filled Point Five Thermo. A comparable down bag would be the Orion from the same manufacturer, while Black's Icelandic range are old favourites. There are, however, many good bags on the market, some of them designed especially for youth groups and adventure centres, which would be adequate. The

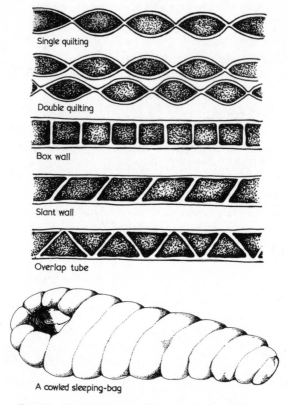

Single quilting

Double quilting

Box wall

Slant wall

Overlap tube

A cowled sleeping-bag

Fig. 19   Sleeping bags: quilting methods and design.

Field and Trek mail order catalogue contains a comprehensive, no-nonsense specification of all the better bags on the market.

Once you've bought a good sleeping-bag, the least you can do is look after it. It shouldn't be allowed to get too dirty before being cleaned and the easiest way to ensure this is to use a sheet sleeping-bag as a liner. You can buy these but they're easily made at home. Use a natural fibre rather than nylon which tends to feel clammy in use. Mine is made from cheesecloth and improves the performance of the bag considerably as well as keeping it clean.

Down bags can usually be dry cleaned but check the label first. They can also be washed by hand with a mild detergent and blown dry with a fan heater on a low setting. Synthetic bags can be thrown into a washing machine, spun dry and hung on the clothes line.

Ground insulation

The problem of sleeping on the ground is not really the hardness so much as the cold. It drains the heat from your body through the compressed filling in the underside of the bag. Even in summer this can make quite a difference to your comfort.

The most popular form of insulation is a closed cell foam mat such as Karrimat. This material is a mere 9mm thick, yet it provides not only first-class insulation but also a surprising degree of comfort. With a dent for your hip kicked in the ground before you pitch the tent, and the foam pad under the groundsheet, where it won't slide around, you can spend a warm and comfortable night. If you like a really soft mattress, though, buy an air-bed.

The more expensive air-beds are heavy, but a cheap PVC one is quite light enough for backpacking. With a sportsman's blanket laid over the top you can do without the insulating foam pad, but by itself an air-bed is not as efficient at keeping you warm owing to the convection currents which your body heat sets up inside it and which carry the heat away. For myself I prefer the sportsman's blanket and air-bed to the Karrimat, but with the trend towards very light, thin groundsheets in modern tents a foam pad under the groundsheet has the added advantage of protecting the tent from wear and tear caused by the rough ground often found in wild country camp sites.

Tents

A tent is more than just a place to sleep. In pitching several tents you establish a community out of nowhere. The psychological impact of this is valuable and easily recognized. A group of expeditioners who are tired, cold, hungry and dispirited so often find morale shooting up again when camp is made and they have what amounts to a home for the night. So never underestimate the Welcome Value of a tent.

This being so, the smallest, lightest backpacking models are not necessarily the most effective. They are, of course, superb all weather shelters, but they're cramped. Better for most purposes is the two- or three-man base camp model which in any case will prove cheaper per head and – if its weight is shared out among all the occupants – probably lighter than most single-man designs.

Single-skin tents have the advantages of lightness, simplicity and low cost, but proofed nylon ones are subject to condensation. Your body moisture collects on the inside and dribbles down the walls. Cotton tents do allow this water vapour to escape through the pores of the fabric while keeping out the relatively coarse rain drops, but they do tend to absorb water and can weigh twice as much when you pack them up after a wet night as they did when dry.

A double-skin tent is not only warmer, working as it does like double glazing, but it combats condensation. The outer skin, or flysheet, is a fully waterproof PU coated nylon but the inner is made from a light cotton or permeable nylon fabric which lets any moisture pass through it. This moisture collects on the underside of the fly and dribbles harmlessly down its sloping sides to the ground outside. Some water can get back into the sleeping area if the inner is accidently pushed against the wet fly but on the whole, and with care, they'll keep you dry in the most adverse conditions.

There are many designs available, some of them very sophisticated. Wedge, pyramid and box shapes with fancy tunnel entrances, snow valances and fiendishly ingenious pole systems, can all be bought but the traditional style of ridge tent with sloping walls meeting at the apex offers good stable accommodation and contains all the features you should be looking for.

The inner tent should have a sewn-in groundsheet extending a few centimetres up the side walls to form a waterproof tray. The side walls themselves should rise vertically for a short distance before sloping in to the roof, as this increases the usable floor space. In the lighter models the floor will taper in width towards the foot, like a sleeping bag, and the roof ridge will slope downwards towards the back as well, further reducing weight and windage.

The flysheet when pitched should sit well clear of the inner and come down to the ground on all sides, so giving complete protection from the elements. At front and back there will probably be bell ends which provide good storage room outside the sleeping area. The back one is usually accessible via a zip from the inner, while the front one forms a complete porch, in which you can change out of wet clothes, stow your rucksack, or even cook – with care – in foul weather.

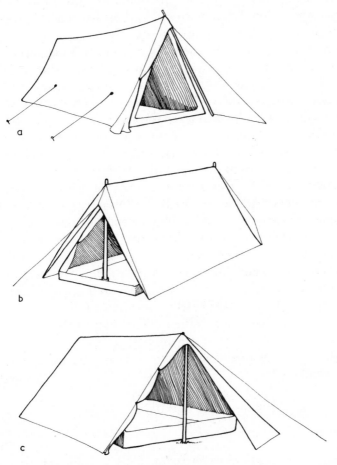

Fig. 20   Tents: (a) Bukta Orienteer tapered ridge with bell end porch; (b) Marechal J/3 Canadian style ridge tent with short front cowl; (c) Ultimate High Country cross ridge with bell ends each side.

Vertical poles are the lightest form of support but A-poles, at least in the front end, will increase stability and make access easier. Often there's a ridge pole to complete the structure, and this does so much to stabilize the tent in windy weather that it's well worth the extra weight. Some form of insect screen and adjustable ventilation on the inner are also useful extras.

Of the many tents which exhibit these features, the Vango Force Ten range which offers a variety of weights and sizes, is probably the best known. Their composite range, with cotton inner and nylon fly are perhaps the best for general purpose expeditioning. Ultimate Equipment Ltd manufacture very high quality tents, and their High Country range are most interesting. These models can be entered from either end and you sleep across the width of the tent – a useful variation which allows you to use the sheltered end as an entrance when the wind changes, and which gives you more elbow room. Robert Saunders manufacture, amongst other good tents, the Basecamp which is a three-man model of similar design with vast storage space in the bell ends. At the cheaper end of the market, but still extremely good, come the Ultimate Tramp, the Saunders Fellpine and the Bukta Orienteer, all of them big enough for two people – if they don't mind it being cosy!

There are even cheaper alternatives in the Canadian style ridge tents, of which the Marechal J/3 is a good robust example. The main difference in style is that the flysheet, while extending to the ground at sides and rear, is open at the front finishing only in a short cowl rather than a full porch. Such a design makes you more vulnerable in bad weather, with the wind being able to get under the flysheet, but if you take care with choosing your site and make sure you pitch the tent tail to the wind it offers good accommodation. I have used this design in winter conditions quite successfully.

Stoves

On the rare occasions when a camp fire is possible you can cook on it but, generally speaking, lightweight stoves are much handier.

Gas stoves are the most common, but least efficient. They're expensive to run, susceptible to draughts, won't burn satisfactorily at low temperatures – and won't burn at all when it's freezing – and they generate less and less heat as the pressure in the canister drops with consumption. Burning time seems to vary with weather conditions so you can't even gauge fuel supply very well. Apart from all this they can be rather unstable with a full pan on top. The Vango ALP 8200, with a liquid feed adapter for cold weather use, overcomes this last problem by siting the canister alongside the burner, while the Epigas Backpacker and the Camping Gaz Globetrotter work better than most. But I have to admit that gas is not my favourite fuel.

I prefer a pressure stove. The classic Primus produces a great deal of heat with a strong, draught resistant flame, using cheap paraffin as fuel. It does need priming with meths or Meta tablets but this is less of a disadvantage than the fact that paraffin stinks. The smell seems to pervade the whole of your pack.

I use a petrol stove since the fuel is universally available, economical to use, burning at about eight hours to the litre, and, being highly volatile, is easier to ignite. You can even use it to prime the stove, which can't be done with paraffin. Contrary to popular belief, it's no more dangerous than gas if used with caution, but petrol stoves do need to be maintained with care or they can become temperamental. The SVEA 123 is a particularly compact model in the well known Optimus range. Their model 88 is perhaps better value with its built-in windshield and cooking pans.

Methylated spirit stoves offer a fourth possibility. The Trangia Stormcooker, marketed by Karrimor, is particularly efficient and comes complete with windshield and pans. It is, however, rather bulky and the temperature cannot be readily regulated. If your budget is really tight an Express Picnic stove is worth considering. These can be bought for pence rather than pounds from most hardware stores and are very basic – just a combined fuel reservoir and burner producing a flame like a gas ring, and a perforated tin cylinder acting as

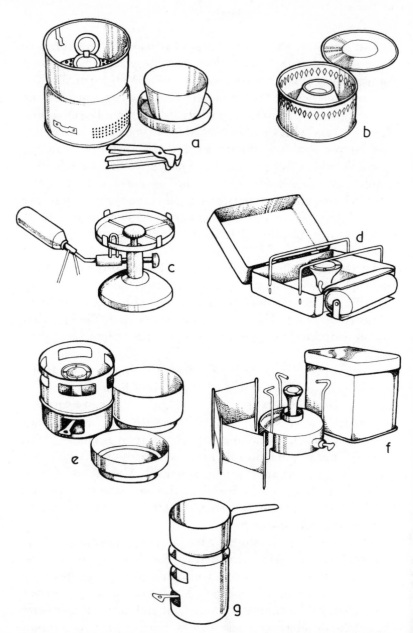

Fig. 21 Light-weight stoves: relative sizes are indicated. (a) Trangia stormcooker:meths; (b) Express Picnic senior size:meths; (c) ALP8200 all-weather liquid feed:gas; (d) Optimus 8R:petrol; (e) Optimus 88:petrol; (f) Optimus 90L:paraffin; (g) SVEA 123:petrol.

windshield and pot stand. All the same, they'll boil $\frac{1}{2}$ litre of water in five minutes and weigh about 56g. They are thirsty, though, burning at around three hours per litre. The heat can't be regulated at all and, as with all meths stoves, you can't see the flame in sunlight. I recently heard of someone trying to refill one, thinking it was out, when it was still burning – with dire consequences.

For lighting your stove, a cheap plastic cigarette lighter is more useful than a box of matches, giving many more lights for the same weight and size, and being less subject to damp or draughts. If you are going to use matches, though, buy the 'strike anywhere' variety and dip each one in melted candle wax. Then put the box in a waterproof container.

Unless your stove has an efficient bult-in windshield, you'll need to shelter it from draughts in use. Finding a naturally sheltered spot isn't always easy and you may find it worth carrying a simple shield like a miniature beach wind-break made from a 60cm by 20cm strip of light cloth with three or four stiff wire struts which stick into the ground.

Utensils

Some of the stoves mentioned above include cooking pans in their design. It's really a matter of personal preference whether you buy such a model or go for separate canteens. The sort of meals you cook, the exact way in which you pack your rucksack and the type of fuel you opt for will all influence your decision. I use an Optimus 8R and a pair of ex-Army mess tins for the simple reason that both items pack neatly into a side pocket of my rucksack, where I can get at them easily for a quick brew-up during the day. These army mess tins are very well made of thicker gauge metal than most modern sets. Cooking pots do take a battering on expedition, and the stronger they are the better. They would, however, be more efficient if fitted with a lid. The handles also have no locking device and can fold up on you just as you're pouring boiling water out of the pan.

There are more popular canteens, such as the Cookwell, which are safer to use but less robust. If you plan to cook in groups of more than two, you'll probably find a set of nesting billies with lids which double as plates the most convenient.

The ideal cooking set for individuals or pairs would consist of a deep lidded pot of about 1 litre capacity and a shallow frying pan, both pan and lid doubling as plates. Such simple combinations seem to be rare, and it may be easier to shop around for cheap cake tins which happen to fit into each other reasonably well and then to buy a bulldog pot-holder, a device, like a pair of pincers, which grips the rim of the pan. They're available from most camping shops.

Some canteens contain sufficient room when nested together to hold at least one day's rations. However, a separate plastic foodbox for each tent is most useful. Apart from keeping all the food together, it can be used as a water bucket, or a washing bowl, as a rubbish bin inside the tent, or even as a small table; and the lid doubles as yet another plate. A 5 litre ice-cream tub is ideal. Anyone with a deep-freezer in their home will probably be able to supply you.

The next items are fuel and water bottles. Fuel being the messy smelly stuff it is, you'd better invest in a proper aluminium screw-top bottle. The seals on these are absolutely tight and the chance of leakage is minimized. It's illegal to carry petrol in a plastic bottle for reasons of safety. The best of these bottles are produced by Sigg and by Optimus.

Water bottles need only be plastic. Most camping and hardware stores can supply wide mouthed screw-capped polythene bottles. The 1 litre size is ideal for water, and the smaller ones can be used to hold things like tea, coffee, sugar and dried milk. A practically free alternative, though liable to crack if handled roughly, is the lightweight type of plastic bottle in which fruit squash is sold. Use the screw capped variety, though, rather than the sort with a flip-top which can spring open with rather dampening consequences.

A drinking mug and some cutlery complete the cooking gear. Aluminium and enamel mugs are not much use. The metal will still be burning your lips when the contents are quite cool. There are insulated plastic beakers on the market, which are perhaps the best choice, giving you a genuinely hot drink when you really need it, but a simple polythene mug is almost as good and even less likely to get broken. For cutlery, lightweight sets of knife, fork and spoon which clip together are the usual choice. However, try managing with just a spoon; you don't really need a fork and you'll already be carrying a pocket or sheath knife, so why duplicate equipment?

Often a knife is carried just for fun, but on a camping expedition as opposed to a day-trek it is a vital tool. You may need it for cutting out turf when digging sanitation holes or preparing fireplaces, preparing kindling, opening tins, sharpening sticks for tent pegs, cooking and eating, so choose it with care. Big sheath knives look good and feel satisfying in use, but wearing one at your waist can be very uncomfortable when you're carrying a pack with a hip belt. The best tool is probably a simple, strong lock-knife with a 10cm blade, but the traditional clasp knife, with a spike and a tin opener, is a useful compromise. Either of these can be carried in a pocket or a lanyard attached to your trouser belt for security. Whatever you use, keep it sharp. A sharp knife is safer than a blunt one, as well as being more useful.

Finally, you'll need a pan cleaner and a sponge. Brillo pads are supposed to spoil aluminium utensils by stripping off the protective oxide coating as well as the grease, but they do get the pans clean. A sponge, in particular a Spontex, is far more practicable than a drying-up cloth. It can also be used for mopping out condensation from inside tents and shell clothing, or wiping the mud off your boots. If you sense a certain lack of hygiene in the variety of uses buy two.

The ditty-bag

The bag itself can be a lightweight day sack, as suggested in Chapter 1, or it can be a dustbin liner, or a special light cotton bag. It's a useful place to keep all the odds and ends so that they don't get scattered around the camp site when you're packing and unpacking. Which of the following items you put in it, or take at all, will depend on your style of camping and choice of equipment so far, but you certainly won't need them all. Think of them as a reserve stock from which to select the items you'll need for any particular trip. It's worth remembering that taking a whole bag full of bits and pieces that *might* come in handy is not only the mark of a novice but adds weight to the pack; every small item counts.

A good torch is essential. It should have enough power to give at least two hours of operational light, just in case you get benighted en route. The flat type which takes a $4\frac{1}{2}$V battery is a good cheap possibility, and you can make it even more useful by improvising a stand for it out of coat-hanger wire. For winter use, though, a head-mounted lamp is best. It leaves your hands free to do things like pitching tents in the dark. The Achil Pile Wonderlamp which can be used as an ordinary torch as well as a headlamp is perhaps the best choice. For anything more than a one-night pitch in mid-summer, you should also pack a spare battery. A spare bulb, carefully protected from breakage in a little cardboard tube, makes for additional peace of mind.

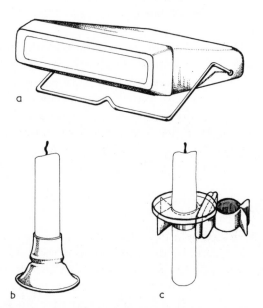

Fig. 22   Lighting: (a) flat torch with home made wire stand clipped into holes in base; (b) candle holder made from baby's bottle teat; (c) Showell Styles' candle holder made from terry clips bolted back to back.

If you want prolonged light, a torch is not really adequate and some form of lantern has to be carried. This poses problems. Paraffin lamps are bulky and tend to leak. Gas lamps, given the limitations of the fuel, are more convenient, but even heavier, as are electric lanterns. This leaves candles, with their potentially lethal naked flame and susceptibility to draughts.

You can use a candle inside a tent, but extreme care is needed, together with a very stable holder. One device described by the eminent writer and backpacker Showell Styles, consists of two terry clips fixed back to back. One holds the candle, the other clips to an upright tent pole. A plastic lid from a food jar with a hole cut in the centre through which the candle is pushed catches the wax. My own alternative, for tents without upright poles, is a teat from the wide-mouthed variety of a baby's feeding bottle. Cut the bulb off the top and push the candle through from the bottom. You end up with a rubber sucker on the end of the candle which, when damped, will stick to the smooth surface on the bottom of a cooking pan.

Next amongst the odds and ends comes the toilet roll. Apart from its intended purpose, soft toilet tissue can be used for wiping the worst of the grease out of a cooking pan and as handkerchiefs; or in a real emergency a brightly coloured roll of it can be unwound along the ground and held down with stones to form a giant SOS for the helicopters.

A small trowel for digging holes, not only in the interests of personal hygiene, but also for burying other organic, bio-degradable rubbish, is most useful. Weight can be saved here by carrying not a proper garden tool but a wide-bladed paint scraper, which does the job just as well.

Personal washing gear can be kept to a minimum. A sliver cut from a bar of soap, a toothbrush, and possibly a comb for your hair are all you need. If washing really becomes unavoidable – and that's how most 'seasoned' expeditioners look at it – you can dry yourself on your general purpose sponge. If you insist on carrying a towel, though, keep to a small one.

On extended expeditions a little dispenser of boot polish,

such as Padawax, is handy for keeping footwear waterproof; and a puncture repair outfit, or even a roll of carpet tape, for air-beds and damaged shell clothing might find a place in the pack. A 'housewife' or sewing kit isn't really necessary; your problem pack (see page 19) will take care of any minor repairs to tent or clothing. Some people suggest taking spare clips and clevis pins for framed packs, and rubber grommets for the tent, but if you checked your gear properly before leaving and you take care of it en route, these shouldn't be needed either.

The problem of stowing kit not required for the moment, and of separating wet or dirty gear from the clean and dry, is solved by packing a dustbin liner. This polythene bag can be filled with anything you want to keep out of the way and left outside the tent whatever the weather. It also doubles as a kneeling mat at the mouth of the tent when the ground is muddy. If you carry a plastic bivvy bag instead of a space blanket, this can be used instead.

For standing camps, where deep grease pits and latrines may need to be dug, a lightweight trenching tool, with folding shovel blade, can be lashed onto the outside of your pack, or strapped into the ice-axe attachment. If you're intending to light fires regularly, a small hand axe can be carried in the same way.

Entertainment is a significant factor to be considered in equipping for an expedition. A good book is always a useful standby, but pack it in a polythene bag to keep it from getting wet. A lighter alternative might be a pack of playing cards, or a travelling set of chess, draughts, solitaire, Mastermind, etc. Finally, a small transistor radio – with earphone, please – can provide solace on wild, wet nights. It's also useful for weather forecasts and news bulletins. Be warned, though, that I, in common with very many others, may take strenuous exception to your radio – and you – if you shatter the peace of a tranquil moor or mountainside with blaring pop.

Spare clothing

If you're properly dressed to begin with you won't need much in the way of spare clothes, but some form of dry rig/sleeping suit is advisable. For summer camping, a sweater and an old pair of trousers, preferably loose, are enough; a track suit is rather better. In winter, by far the best garment is the fibre-pile suit, described on page 16. Worn straight over cellular underwear, even in the coldest weather, the feeling is one of luxurious warmth.

Summer or winter, spare socks should be carried so that the ones on your feet can have a chance to air, and dry out if necessary. One pair of each type that you're wearing is sufficient. One set of spare underwear also makes for comfort on extended expeditions.

By no means essential, but very convenient in a standing camp, is a pair of light shoes. In dry weather plimsolls are ideal and, in the wet, a pair of short wellingtons, or even galoshes if you can get them. If you can't, you might consider cutting off an old pair of wellingtons at the ankles. They should, naturally, be of a size to fit your feet with the full complement of socks.

The virtue of having spare lightweight shoes is that when you want to go out of your tent, it's much easier to slip these on than it is to don and lace up walking boots. In any case, it makes a pleasant change after several days of wearing full-weight leather, and gives tired feet a new lease of life when wandering around camp at the end of a long trek.

6 Lightweight camping

Planning the expedition

In organizing a camping expedition the preparations you make for a simple day-trek still apply but there are more things to think about. First, you have to remember that you'll probably be walking three times as far, even if you're camping out for only one night. In addition, your pack could weigh three times as much. By its very nature, a camping expedition will take you into wilder country which means more difficult terrain.

All this adds up to the fact that you must pace yourself carefully upon the trail. Rest times will increase in frequency and length, totalling ten or fifteen minutes per hour in mountainous areas. Steady progress throughout the day should bring you to your camp site with at least an hour of daylight left – until you're experienced enough to make camp in the dark, anyway. And on an extended expedition you'll have to plan the route so as to touch on places where you can restock with supplies when necessary.

Having chosen the area for the expedition, you'll have some idea of the routes you could follow so search the map for suitable camping areas before finalizing the details. What you're looking for at this point is somewhere for which you can obtain prior permission, or where the privilege of being allowed to put up your tent has been established by general usage. Choosing the actual 5m sq plot is covered later in this chapter.

Obtaining permission to camp, either by contacting the landowner before setting off, or seeking him out when you arrive, is officially the correct practice, but it's not as easy as it sounds; some research will be necessary. If you want to use official camp sites you'll find them marked on tourist maps. The head offices of the National Park Planning Boards, whose addresses can be obtained from The Countryside Commission (see Appendix 1), can supply details of the ownership of access land. Adventure and outdoor education centres in the area can give advice, and mountain or tourist information centres are worth consulting, as are the police or, where appropriate, the coastguard, and of course the local farmers. The alternative is to pay a visit to the camping area beforehand and enquire from anyone you can find.

This last possibility is often cited as an essential part of preparation. For the leader of a large party, it is; but for a small group of young people out to enjoy themselves in their own time, it's not always practicable, and as much second-hand local knowledge as possible should therefore be gained from guide books and other campers before setting off.

Camping on open moorland and beside public rights of way is usually discouraged, both for reasons of safety and because of the pressure on the ecology of the area caused by incompetent campers. Such areas can be used, but tact and discretion are needed. As an expeditioner, you must remember that it's up to you to prove that camping 'wild' in this overcrowded land can still be permitted without risk to the countryside. Otherwise the time will come – indeed it's nearly here, as the anti-tourist fences on Snowdon will testify – when, like the very sheep, we're tagged, herded, and even fleeced for the privilege.

Nobody likes to admit it, but in fact, a great many campers pitch their tents discreetly and unofficially, without the knowledge of the landowner. I don't propose to comment on this practice further than to say that experience will tell you just how far to follow the official line. It's worth remembering, though, that farmers have a living to make, and your camp site is very much their business.

Food

Equally as important as knowing where you'll be laying your head for the night is being able to look forward to your food. To keep going in wild country you need to eat three or four thousand calories a day. If this seems a lot, consider that the energy in a lump of sugar will sustain you for an hour while sitting watching television but will burn up in eight seconds when you're climbing a steep slope with a 13kg pack on your back.

About half the food should be carbohydrate, the rest being split equally between fat and protein; the vitamins will all come naturally. The sorts of foods to consider include honey or brown sugar, dried fruit, chocolate, peanuts, soft margarine – which comes in convenient tubs and spreads in cold weather – cheese, crackers or hard-tack biscuits, porridge oats and muesli, instant mashed potato mix, eggs, tinned or freeze-dried meat, freeze-dried vegetables, Oxo cubes, instant soups, tea-bags, coffee powder and dried or condensed milk. Anyone who's been on a diet can probably quote you the calorific value per 25g for every one of these, and calorie counting booklets can readily be bought in most stationers.

Freeze-dried foods are obviously the easiest and lightest to carry. Tins are so much wasted weight, on the whole, though some things, like corned beef and creamed rice, are useful. Vesta meals can be bought from most supermarkets, though their portions do tend to be on the small side and they take a long while to cook. Batchelors market dried meat dishes and vegetables in twelve-portion catering packs, obtainable from cash-and-carry stores, and Kelloggs now market several dried products, including 'Rise and Shine' fruit juice powder, which I never go without.

Really no more expensive, and yet produced especially for lightweight campers and backpackers, are the expedition rations marketed by Raven and by Springlow. These consist of complete meals packed with flavour and calories, and cooked in a few minutes using a single pan. You can buy them in camping shops but Springlow also run a mail order service. Their address is in Appendix 1. Of particular interest are their sweetened oatmeal blocks, which can be eaten like biscuits or made into porridge, and their fortified service hard-tack biscuits.

Meal times tend to be flexible on expedition; you eat when you're hungry and when you find a convenient spot. When buying in your provisons, though, it's convenient to plan a rough menu in terms of breakfast, lunch and tea. For a day's eating it might read something like the following:

Breakfast Tea or coffee. Muesli or porridge. Scrambled egg (Raven products). Hard-tack and margarine with jam. Stewed fruit. More tea or coffee.

Lunch Instant soup. Hard-tack and margarine with cheese. Raisins. Chocolate biscuits (Penguins).

Trail snacks Fruit juice (Kelloggs 'Rise and Shine'). Mars bars. Kendal Mint Cake. Peanuts.

Tea Chicken risotto (Springlow). Rice pudding. Tea or coffee and chocolate biscuits. Last thing before brushing your teeth: drinking chocolate and handful of raisins.

Actually, if you get through this lot you might well be considered a greedy person. As you gain experience you can cut out the items that you find you're not eating but, to begin with, when your expeditions are short enough anyway for the total weight of food not to be unmanageable, it's worth erring on the greedy side.

Allowing one canteen and one food box per two-man tent, you should be able to pack it all in, but strip off any fancy packaging first and portion the food out into polythene sandwich bags. Do label them clearly. It always makes me laugh when novices whiten their coffee with potato powder but, for some reason, they never find it funny.

Finally, remember the purifying tablets. It is always advisable to purify water if you camp below habitations or near livestock. The easiest way is to use Puritabs, obtainable from chemists. Full instructions are included with the packs, and if you make the tea strong you won't taste the chlorine.

Packing

Once your rations are assembled in their containers, it's time to get together the rest of your gear. Having decided on what you'll be taking, make up your own check list. You will, in fact, find one such list at the end of this book, but use it simply as a rough guide. The purpose of the check list is partly so that you don't leave anything essential behind, but preparing it also makes you consider the use and value of every item; hence the need for thinking out your own list, rather than copying blindly.

Now comes the exciting bit: putting it all in the pack. In order to achieve the best balance the gear which is lightest for its size should go at the bottom and the heaviest at the top, against the inside of the back panel, next to your shoulder blades. However, some compromise will be necessary. Some items you'll want frequently throughout the day: for example, your stove, brew-up ingredients, and possibly your warm wear, and you don't want to find yourself having to empty the pack all over a mountainside just to reach them.

The exact order in which you pack will vary with the style of sack, the nature of the contents and the type of expedition, but the following system, offered as a general guide, works well in most circumstances.

In the case of framed packs, the foam insulating pad, if carried, is rolled up and strapped onto the frame underneath the sack. A variation is to put it, rolled up more loosely, into a waterproof stuff bag and then squeeze your sleeping-bag into the hole in the middle. With anatomic and frameless sacks, the foam mat is coiled vertically round the inside as a waterproof liner, all the rest of the gear being packed inside the void with the sleeping-bag at the bottom.

In sacks with a double main compartment, the sleeping bag goes at the bottom of the upper one. The lower compartment is occupied by spare clothes including warm wear, and hat and gloves when not being worn. On top of the sleeping-bag is placed the food box; next to it goes the ditty-bag containing all the odds and ends except the torch. The air-bed, if carried, is folded flat and slid down between these two items and the back panel.

The tent can be kept in its own bag and pushed under the top flap of the rucksack, but with the trend towards shaped lids, it's often better to stow it inside. In this case poles are stowed vertically through the corner holes in the platform separating upper and lower compartments. The flysheet and the pegs in their own little bag lie on top of the ditty-bag and the inner tent is folded into a flat parcel to form the next layer.

Next comes any specialist gear you might be carrying, such as a coiled walking rope, slings and karabiners. Then comes the stove and canteen, containing, ideally, lunch and brew-up ingredients. You'll definitely want these during the day, so if they'll fit into a side pocket so much the better. One variation is to sling the coiled rope over your shoulder, but I prefer to get everything into the pack if I can.

The main sack is then closed and shell clothing is folded up and placed on top, under the lid. In the case of undivided sacks, warm wear can also be carried here. In the outside pockets go fuel and water bottles, mug, spoon, toilet roll and trowel, sportsman's blanket or bivvy bag if carried in preference to a space blanket, torch, lighter or matches – unless you prefer to carry these on your person – maps not immediately required, and your notebook. Anything else, such as camera, film, suntan cream and lipsalve, which will definitely be wanted during the day's walking, should also be squeezed in here.

In my own anatomic sack, the food box goes into the left-hand side of the upper main compartment and the ditty-bag on the right. Stove and mess tins occupy the left-hand outer pocket while the heavier fuel and water bottles, together with mug, cutlery and trail snacks are packed into the right-hand pocket. Mixing food and fuel hasn't caused any problems yet, but I do use a Sigg fuel bottle with a first-class screw cap. All the other items fit into the big lid pocket. The result is a well balanced pack, with everything to hand when I want it.

The only item which should be strapped onto the outside of the pack is your ice-axe. Skis, crampons and technical climbing hardware also go here, of course, but you haven't got to the stage where you require these. Water bottles, frying pans, mugs, and so on, dangling around and banging about are an abomination.

When you're trekking with a group much of this gear can be shared out. He who takes the food box, for example, won't be carrying the tent. This makes for a lighter pack, of course. I've seen young expeditioners with communal gear shared between three of them set off for three days with packs weighing less than 10kg apiece, so you may rest assured that being well equipped doesn't have to break your back. With your rucksack packed as recommended above, you should be able to trek all day and still put a spring into your step as you walk into your chosen camp site.

Making camp

First of all, forget everything you may have been told about the 'ideal camp site'. There's no such thing but there are some basic considerations which determine whether a site is habitable or not.

With modern tents, shelter from the prevailing wind may be desirable, but it's not essential. Dry, level ground is rather more important. Bear in mind that ground which is dry when you arrive may turn into a quagmire when it rains if the surrounding area drains into it. Camping in sheltered hollows or at the foot of a protecting slope should be considered with caution in changeable weather. Apart from the danger of flooding, low-lying ground is usually colder at night than any pitch higher up the slope, since the cool night air drains into the valleys. Morning mist can also hang around the hollows.

Best, then, is a patch of level ground a little higher than the surrounding area and open to the early morning sunshine but backed by a wall, rock outcrop or belt of wind-breaking natural growth. Running water, suitable for drinking, after purification if necessary, is handy but not essential if you ration yourself carefully to the supply in your water bottles.

Try to avoid camping too near bracken, nettle beds and marshy areas if you don't like sharing your tent with a couple of million insects. Avoid closed fields occupied by livestock. On the open moor they cause no problem, but in a restricted space they tend to regard intruders with too intimate an interest.

Finally test the ground to see if the tent pegs will go in. On poor ground the holes can be started with the marlin spike on a clasp knife, and in the last resort pegs can be backed up with, or even replaced by, heavy stones, but none of these can beat a simple tent peg pushed well home in gravel, clay or good firm peat. How to pitch a tent on tough ground is covered on pages 119–21.

Having picked the spot for your tent clear the ground completely of stones, tussocks, cowpats, and any other rubbish that could damage the groundsheet or cause uncomfortable lumps. Flatten dead stubble carefully, and lay dead bracken fronds or handfuls of grass over any patches of bare earth. This helps insulation and keeps the groundsheet clean.

The most obvious thing to do now is pitch the tent, but I prefer first to find a sheltered spot for the stove or rig the windshield, and get a brew on. It's worth taking trouble to ensure that your kitchen is convenient. You need a flat area not only for the stove but for pans, bottles and packets of food; and it shouldn't be too far from where the tent will stand or the cook feels isolated. If you do this job now, then by the time the tent is pitched there'll be a cup of tea or soup waiting which will keep you going until the other chores are done and the meal is cooked. This is always good practice, and when you're tired it's a significant safety factor. It gives you the will and energy to make your camp secure.

It's a matter of safety as well as pride that your tent should be pitched quickly. You could need the shelter in a hurry one day, so practise the routine. First assemble the poles and lay them to hand with the pegs. Second spread out the foam pads, if carried, and unroll the inner tent on top of them, rear towards the prevailing wind, and peg out the corners of the groundsheet ensuring that the door is closed to discourage insects from entering and to help the tent keep its shape. Once the tent is secure from being blown away you can peg out the rest of the groundsheet without having to struggle.

The poles should now be set up in position. With internal poles you'll have to open the tent doors, but close them again as soon as you've finished. Setting up the front pole first makes reaching into the tent to position the back one much easier. There should be two little foot plates to go under the poles;

don't forget them! Temporarily guy the tent, or fit the ridge pole if there is one and stand back to look. Adjust pegs and tensions to get the tent sitting fair and taut.

All is now ready for the flysheet. Start at the rear of the tent and let any wind that's around do the work by blowing the flysheet out horizontally over the tent as you hold it by its edge. Having carefully manouevred the flysheet into position over the rear pole peg it down securely at the back and get up front quickly before it damages itself by flapping around. Peg it down at the front and then go round and secure it on all sides, corners first.

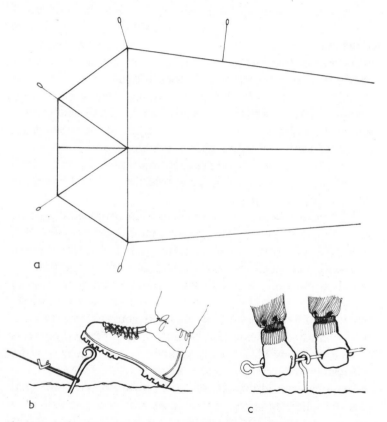

Fig. 23 Fixing tent pegs: (a) guys should bisect angle of fabric at point of attatchment; (b) insert pegs by hand or steady pressure of boot; (c) lift stubborn pegs with spare used as lever – never pull up by guys.

The rule with all pegs is to push them into the hilt by hand or steady pressure from your boot; never hammer them in, unless you like your pegs bent. They should be set at 45° to the vertical, with heads pointing away from the tent. Any tension you put on guys or peg points should be gentle and in a direction which bisects the angle formed with the fabric at the point of attachment.

The real knack of tent pitching lies in less obvious points, such as ensuring that empty peg, pole and flysheet bags are weighted down with stones to keep them from blowing away, putting pegs down carefully in a pile to avoid losing any, and extending guy lines to their full length wherever possible to improve set and stability. The wrinkles and flutters you so often see on nylon tents aren't necessary. It's just a matter of selecting and preparing the site carefully and taking some trouble with putting the thing up.

In really wild weather the whole exercise can be rather hectic, so don't worry about appearance initially, but go round making adjustments once all the pegs are in (anyway, see page 115). Whatever the circumstances, though, do try and take a pride in pitching your tent well; and before you go any further, do have that cup of tea.

Living arrangements

Having finished your hot drink you can set about making yourself at home. If you're in a group, cooks will have been appointed, preferably one for each tent, and they should be allowed to get on with the job undisturbed. If you're on your own, you can start the meal cooking and then turn to the other work.

Air-beds, if carried, should be inflated and positioned in the tent. Sleeping-bags can be unpacked, shaken and laid out with tops turned over to keep out the bugs. Doing this now allows them to air a little and loft well before use. Any other items that you'll need, such as torch, candle, washing gear, warm wear and so on, should be stowed handy in the tent, near the entrance. Assuming the weather's fine – and it should be for your first trip – you need not crawl around inside the tent again until you retire for the night. Observing this rule ensures that it stays tidy!

Next comes the digging of a grease pit. As with all holes you dig, start by removing the turf carefully and laying it on one side for replacing when you leave. For a one- or two-night pitch the pit need be no more than a shallow scoop in the ground. Some solo backpackers don't even bother with this much but I think it's better at least to lift the turf before scraping your plates onto the ground. Theoretically, there shouldn't be any wasted food to scrape, but, while you're learning camp cooking, there will be. The hole should be sited near the kitchen, or it won't get used, but don't put it in any place where someone could stumble into it.

The pit should contain only organic, bio-degradable rubbish. If you're not going to have a camp fire save all combustible waste until you leave, put it into the pit last thing before you go and set it alight. Then you can fill in the pit on top of the ashes. It's worth remembering that if you do have a good hot camp fire going, practically all waste will burn. Even tins can be laid in the embers, after which they'll be clean and soft enough to flatten and fold up very small for carrying to the nearest rubbish bin.

If you're staying at the camp site for more than one night select a spot a little way from the tents and where there's some natural screening for use as a toilet area. Another pit can be dug and a trowel left with the pile of earth. After each use earth should be sprinkled into the pit; and again, it should all be filled in when you leave. For a one-night pitch, or when you're on your own, it's sufficient just to lift a square of turf or a half-buried rock. Hardened backpackers who scoff at such niceties should try camping wild in Germany – if they can find an unpolluted coppice, ditch or hedgerow in which to lay their sleeping bags.

Camp fires

Whenever it's possible a camp fire offers a marvellous focal point for the group, particularly if there's more than one tent, but do remember the very first rule of the Country Code (to be found in full at the end of this book). Guard against all risk of fire. Remember, too, that apart from any risk to the countryside, fires seem directly or indirectly to be the cause of most camping accidents. One young lad in a group I took camping once ended up in Dartmoor Prison – the nearest place where he could get stitches put into a finger he'd nearly chopped off while preparing firewood.

The site for the fireplace should be downwind of the tents and far enough away for sparks to have no chance of jumping on to the fabric. It need not be visible from the tent entrance, since you don't retire for the night without dousing it. There are numerous styles of fireplace, each one supposedly ideal for its job – cooking, drying clothes, or just providing warmth. The type I find most versatile is prepared as follows.

Remove a 60cm square of turf, or scoop out earth for a depth of about 5cm. This will be replaced when you leave. Line the edge of the hole with stones to protect the surrounding ground, and now collect a plentiful supply of firewood. Never cut it from standing trees, even if they look dead – they're still part of the landscape. Dry wood can be found under bushes and hedges if you look for it whatever the weather; and damp wood can be persuaded to burn if you shave curling splinters from it, so that they stand out from the surface. Anything much thicker than 5cm, though, won't burn well in the size of fire we're thinking of, however dry it is.

When it comes to lighting a fire, don't be a purist. Dry leaves and grass, the traditional kindling, are extremely difficult to use. The best natural fire lighter is the papery surface of birch bark, which can be peeled off the tree without damaging it, and will burn fiercely even when soaking wet. A couple of Meta tablets, however, weigh practically nothing and make life much easier, so carry some in your pack. Never use paraffin, petrol, or even meths: sooner or later you'll blow yourself up.

The procedure is to make in the centre of your fireplace a small wigwam of your thinnest sticks – pencil size is about right – over the Meta tablets. Add a few thicker sticks to the wigwam to give the fire something to feed on, but don't pile on too much. Fuel should be added as the flames increase, retaining the pyramidal shape for as long as possible, as this produces a chimney effect which draws the flames up. Once the fire's burning well you can let it die down a little to form glowing coals; add just enough fuel to keep it that way and you'll have bright warmth without smoke or flying sparks over which you can dry clothes suspended on long sticks, and round which you can sit without being kippered or singed.

Fig. 24   The camp fire: note that turf is folded, grass inwards, and stacked neatly for replacement.

When you've finished with the fire and the fireplace, pour water onto the embers, slowly and taking care to cover the whole area. Go on soaking the ashes until no wisp of steam remains. Then stamp the ashes flat, return the stones to the places from which they came and replace the earth or turf. Scatter any remaining fuel where you found it and remove all chips and splinters of wood from the area of the fireplace. No evidence whatever should be left.

Cooking

Cooking freeze-dried and convenience foods is easy enough. The packs in which you buy them always give instructions. Read these before transferring the contents to polythene bags, and if you can't remember them, cut them out and slip them in with the food. Boiling food is much the best method, being simple, quick and clean. Frying leaves you with greasy pans and, when cooking inside the tent in wild weather, introduces the risk of spitting fat burning holes in the canvas and the cook.

If it's possible, turning down the flame of the stove or holding the pan somewhat above it will prevent food burning and making the pan difficult to clean. Using lids at all times will speed the process and conserve fuel. Getting everything quite ready before you light the stove will also save a lot of time and trouble, and careful, deliberate movement will minimize the chance of accidents.

With organization it's possible to cook even a three-course meal on a single-burner stove without there having to be a wait between courses. As soon as the first hot drink has been made, boil up another pan of water for the instant soup and the vegetables. When this is ready, place the pan containing the main course on the stove and cover it with the one containing the water. If vegetables are to be cooked separately from the main dish, rather than thrown in with it, put them into the hot water now to soak. They'll require very little further cooking by the time the main dish is ready. The soup and mashed potato can be made by straining off some of the water when required. It should be quite hot enough, and any vegetable flavouring will add seasoning and conserve vitamins!

When the main course is cooked swap the pans over to finish off the vegetables if necessary, make the soup and summon the group to eat. By the time the soup is drunk you should be ready to strain off the remaining vegetable water to make the mashed potato which you can do while someone else is sharing out the main dish. Vegetables and potato dished up, you can then wipe out the pan and refill it with the pudding, to be heated while you are eating, or with enough water for the after dinner coffee and any washing up necessary. Hot water for the latter is no luxury, and is well worth a small amount of fuel. With a hot pudding on the menu, of course, the coffee/washing up water can be heating while that is being eaten.

Finally, if there's stewed fruit or porridge for breakfast the main dish pan can be washed or wiped clean and these items heated up before being allowed to soak overnight. In the morning the fruit will be beautifully tender, and the porridge smooth and creamy, each requiring only a few minutes' heating. This trick of leaving food to soak is also useful in standing camps. You can prepare the evening meal after breakfast, thus cutting the cooking time when you return to camp tired and hungry. Even more ingenious is the use of a 'haybox'. For the lightweight expeditioner, this means wrapping the pan up in a sleeping-bag to keep the heat in and let the food cook in its own juice while you're away from camp.

The whole process need take no longer than three-quarters of an hour, and it's fun. If you don't like cooking, though, don't worry. Raven and Springlow Sales both produce special meal packs that cook in five minutes or less. In any case, the sort of meal described above is really for gourmets and show-offs. To begin with you're best advised to keep it really simple. If you're ambitious as a cook practise first at home. You may very well change your mind.

Getting comfortable

In a lightweight camp gadgets are more of a complication than a help. Apart from using the nylon line in your problem pack or the walking rope if you're carrying one, as a clothes line, it's best to avoid gimmicks. Clothes lines, though, are useful for airing as well as drying clothes and sleeping-bags, particularly in the morning when you can't drape things over the ridge of the tent because the fabric is wet with dew. Don't set it up between the poles of two tents; it needs to be fairly taut to keep the clothes draped on it clear of the ground, and consequently it puts an unfair strain on the tent. It is better to stretch it between trees, rocks or bushes. If you double it and twist it together clothes can be secured by poking them through a couple of twists.

Good camping is very much a matter of thinking ahead. A camp in which the tents are pitched as close together as possible always seems cosy, but you find that as you walk around you trip over all the guy ropes. It's therefore advisable to mark them by tying a bunch of bracken or grass round them. You can even use the versatile toilet tissue.

Except in the driest weather, a standing camp soon begins to develop muddy paths winding through it, with a particularly soggy patch at the entrance to each tent. Taking care to vary the route from point to point around the camp site will help; and the polythene dustbin liner can also be laid out flat in the porch of each tent to make a sitting or kneeling mat.

Before wriggling into your sleeping-bag place your torch to hand, along with something to eat in case you wake up hungry in the middle of the night. Stove, mugs, hot drink ingredients and a pan full of water should be set out at the entrance to the tent so that the cook can make the first brew-up of the day without having to get fully out of his sleeping-bag. For the same reason, it's worth sleeping with your head towards the door. Any clothes you take off can be folded carefully to make a pillow. Air-beds with pillows built in still need covering with fabric, unless your head is buried in a hooded sleeping bag, or you'll wake up with your face sticking to the plastic.

Comfortable sleeping arrangements are most important. If you're not using an air-bed it's worth lying down on your insulating mat even before you pitch the tent. Wriggle around until you find all the bumps in the ground, then remove them. Make hollows for hips and shoulders, or build up the area around your waist. In bad weather, of course, this can't be done, but make as comfortable a mattress as possible with anything and everything to hand as soon as you're inside the tent.

Unless the weather is very cold, strip off as much clothing as possible before going to bed. The sleeping-bag filling lofts as your body heat expands the air in it. Wearing full clothing can, in fact, prevent your body heat from radiating sufficiently to do this, and you can feel colder than if you strip off. Fibre-pile clothing doesn't seem to have quite the same effect and can increase comfort in very cold weather. Before resorting to this, though, don socks, gloves and balaclava. The latter, particularly, makes a great deal of difference. If you do sleep fully clothed you'll just have to put up with feeling chilly when you climb out of your bag in the morning. Resist the temptation to pile on more clothing over the top. The tendency is to keep it on even when you set off for the day, with the result that you cook. It's a foolish practice, if you think about it, but I've seen many novices guilty of it.

Stripping to the skin, giving clothes a thorough shake, and getting dressed again feels almost as good as a bath after a couple of days on expedition. There's also a definite psychological advantage to changing into your dry rig when you've finished making camp even if your trail clothes are still dry and reasonably clean. Remember, though: it is a dry rig, so keep it that way.

Insects are a fact of life when camping in fine weather, and some sort of repellent is useful. Proprietary creams can be bought but this is one more item to be carried, and for short expeditions there is another trick which doesn't work for everyone but is worth trying. Last thing before setting out drink a tumblerful of water containing a tablespoonful of vinegar. Cider vinegar is more palatable than the ordinary malt variety. For the next twenty-four hours or so your skin should be slightly acidic, and this puts the insects off.

One of the most rewarding dodges for camping in fine weather is that of doing without a tent. Until you've slept beneath an open sky, you'll never really know what wild country's all about. Some precautions against a change in the weather are sensible, though.

The simplest routine is to lay out a sportsman's blanket or a polythene sheet over an insulating mat with half the blanket lying to one side of it. If you lie down in your sleeping-bag on the half covering the mat the remainder of the blanket is ready to be folded over the top of you, should you be woken by rain. A couple of tent pegs or heavy stones laid ready to hand can be used to secure the corners of the cover, so that it stays in place when you turn over, or if there's any wind. An alternative is to lie on top of a bivvy bag, and to crawl into it if necessary. The lack of ventilation in these things, however, can make for a sticky night.

Finally, of course, you can cheat. Refer to page 135 then lie back and look at the stars through a protective roof of transparent polythene.

Striking camp

All too often with an inexperienced group, the second day of an expedition gets off to a bad start simply because too much time is wasted before setting out. The camp site which took perhaps half an hour to set up the previous night seems to take three hours to break. Not only does time on the trail become severely limited, but rucksacks are inefficiently packed, items are lost, plans for the day which have had to be revised in the light of the lack of time are imperfectly prepared, and everybody sets off feeling vaguely frustrated and wishing secretly that they were going straight home.

To avoid all this a routine is essential. And, as always, a deliberate effort should be made to indulge yourself with a little comfort and enjoyment. For example, the morning can start with tea in bed. The cook of the day, if he isn't awake when the rest of the tent stirs, can be kicked into action. If everything was properly prepared the night before he need not get out of his sleeping-bag. Enjoying a hot drink while you're warm and comfortable provides an opportunity for planning exactly who will do what and in what order, to make striking camp a quick and painless exercise.

You can then dress, one at a time. Resist the temptation to put on your trail clothes over the top of whatever you slept in unless it was just your underwear, or you'll have no reserve of dry clothing should it be needed later in the day. Sleeping-bags should be turned inside out and hung to air on the clothes line or draped over the tent, nearby rocks or bushes if they're not still wet with dew. The same can be done with your dry rig.

While the cook is preparing breakfast you can deal with the personal chores, such as washing, tidying away personal odds and ends of gear, or giving boots a clean and a coat of polish.

Breakfast over and washing up done, it's time to sit down with another cup of tea and finalize the plans for the day. Everyone in the group will, of course, know what the proposed routes or activities are, but weather conditions, the fitness of the group and the cold grey light of the second day on the trail can all dictate a change of mind – within the limitations of the problems discussed on pages 45–7.

If the camp is to remain standing while you go out on a day-trek all gear should be neatly stowed inside the tents and the camp site left immaculate. Sleeping bags should be packed into their stuff bags since they will otherwise get damp, even inside the tent, in humid weather. As you'll require only one small pot for brewing up during the day you can even prepare the evening meal and leave it in the remaining pans, to be heated up on your return. Finally pack day sacks and zip shut tents.

If you're striking camp there's rather more to do. First, every scrap of litter should be removed, burnt if possible, dumped in the grease pit if organic, or put in a polythene bag for taking away. The fireplace and all remaining fuel should be removed, and the toilet and grease pits filled in.

Next comes the packing of rucksacks, as far as possible while the tents are still up. Striking the tents should be the very last job. Obviously, their shelter can be useful when packing, and should be retained for as long as possible in threatening weather, but the main reason for leaving them until all the other jobs are done is that unless everyone is concentrating on this one job, tent, flysheet and poles get scattered around owing to interruptions; you forget who's carrying which part of which tent in his rucksack, items are left inside tents, only to be discovered when you try to roll it up; pegs disappear, and so on.

Finally, make a thorough ground-check, examining the whole area minutely for any forgotten items or removable traces of your presence. A few hours after you've gone, when the flattened grass has had a chance to pick itself up, no one should know that you passed that way.

When you first go camping, you'll probably be up and about by 6am. As you gain experience in making yourself comfortable, you'll sleep longer, but, given that to make the most of your day you should leave the site no later than 9am, getting-up time shouldn't be postponed much beyond 7 o'clock.

Camping is a discipline as well as an art. To be successful you have to think ahead and become slightly fanatical about tidiness and being organized. Following the routines outlined in this chapter will help you to achieve the basic standard without which your camp will collapse in the first brush with bad weather or when the terrain is difficult.

7 Frontier camping

Camping in rain

The title of this chapter might seem rather whimsical, but it refers not only to camping in the wildest areas but also in conditions which test your skill, your resolution and your equipment to their limits. And the British climate being what it is, the first test you're likely to experience is rain. There's nothing more guaranteed to reduce a camper and his gear to a pulp than a persistent downpour, and yet there's no reason why he shouldn't stay dry and comfortable.

If the tent you're using is such that the fly can be pitched first, or if it can be modified to make this possible, you can pitch the fly and pile in under it while you sort yourself out. Even if the inner tent has to be pitched first it shouldn't be exposed to the rain for long enough to get seriously wet if you've practised the routine explained in the last chapter.

Having pitched the tent forget about all the chores, such as digging grease pits, laying out kitchens and airing sleeping bags. In doing without these refinements you'll have to take special care with keeping gear tidy and storing rubbish for later disposal. Once again, routine is all-important.

Open the tent entrance, lay your pack down with its top flap just inside the tent, take off your cagoule and fold it so as to protect the inside from getting wet and lay it on top of the pack where it will stay clean. Drop your over trousers till the waistband is just above your knees and then sit down inside the entrance of the tent. The whole business takes about thirty seconds so your unprotected top half will be barely damp and the inside of your tent stays clean and dry. Your lower legs are still protected and can stay out in the rain for as long as you care to leave them there. Your pack is accessible from inside the tent, without its dropping water all over the groundsheet, and is also protected by the cagoule from getting any wetter.

Now stow fuel bottle, stove, food, water and utensils under the flysheet on one side of the entrance. Bring everything else you need for this one night into the tent. Put the rest of your gear, including the rucksack itself, inside your polythene dustbin liner and secure the top carefully. You can now leave it outside quite happily. In the morning you can shake the worst of the water off the polybag before turning it inside out for stowing inside the pack.

Overtrousers and boots can now be taken off and put, with the cagoule, under the fly on the side opposite the cooking gear. Remember that the inside of the fly will get wet with condensation, so stow these items so that their own insides are protected. Take off socks, if they're wet, and any other clothes that are soaked, and wring them out if necessary before folding them into the smallest possible bundle for placing in one corner of the inner tent ready to dry a little over the stove later. Clothing that is merely damp will soon dry on you so keep wearing it for the moment, and change into dry rig when all the sorting out has been done.

Lose no further time in getting fully inside the tent. And having done that, stay there. The whole secret, really, is to remain 'indoors' from the first time you get inside. Assuming that the tent is properly pitched and that fly and groundsheet are waterproof, there's no way water or mud can get in without your going outside to fetch it.

It's also essential that you're meticulously tidy. The tendency, not only of novices but of some experienced expeditioners I know, is to clutter the tent with gear. Things then have to be moved in and out, a sort of wrestling match ensues, and something – usually the routine – has to give way. So furnish the tent very carefully. Choose a place for everything and make sure it stays there. Then change into dry rig and fold trail clothes into a neat bundle at the head of your bed. In very cold weather bring your boots inside, too, or they'll freeze during the night.

There are also one or two other chores which mustn't be

neglected. Most important is the control of condensation. When the atmosphere outside is saturated condensation inside will be even worse than usual, so try and keep the tent as well ventilated as possible without letting the rain in. If it's pitched tail-to-wind you ought to be able to leave the doors open, but don't let yourself get too cold.

In addition, make sure that the sponge is laid handy. Whenever moisture appears, mop it up and squeeze the sponge outside the door. Most water will collect on the groundsheet in a double-skinned tent, but those with light nylon rather than cotton inners are also likely to drip on you from the canopy.

The inside of the fly will be streaming, so take care not to push the inner against it. The greatest risk of this happening occurs when you roll over in your sleep during the night and when two people are trying to move about at once. To eliminate the first cause, one camper I know places some hard-cornered piece of gear between himself and the tent: if he does roll over onto it, it soon wakes him up. When awake, move one at a time, slowly, methodically, and as little as possible. Camping in the wet can really be quite relaxing.

From the point of view of staying dry, falling snow can be treated as rain. Even more care has to be taken with condensation as the weather will probably be too cold for the tent to be fully ventilated, and you may also be resorting to artificial heating in the form of stoves and candles, both of which emit copious quantities of water – along with fumes from the burnt fuel. And the fumes themselves create some risk. Tents aren't usually so airtight that a massive build-up of noxious gases can be formed easily, but be on the alert for this danger, and don't burn stoves inside closed tents for long periods.

Providing that the weight of snow settling on the fly isn't enough to press it against the inner, you can leave it there – it improves the insulation of the tent. But again, be on the alert and knock it off, if necessary, by slapping the inside of the tent briskly wherever there's a connecting point between inner and fly. This way, the movement will transmit itself to the outside without your actually pushing the two skins together. Pitching tents on already fallen snow is covered later in this chapter.

Striking camp in wet weather is the exact reverse of the procedure for making camp in rain, explained above. The tent will be wet and the groundsheet probably muddy so don't put it in your pack or it'll soak the contents. You'll be wearing your shell clothing by the time you come to strike, so strap the tent in its place, under the lid but with the main compartment closed by pulling the draw-cord tight.

There is another possibility, though, when you wake up to find the rain dribbling soggily out of a sky like a wet dishcloth: turn over and go back to sleep. Or at least, having dressed, breakfasted and tidied up the tent, stay inside and rest up for a couple of hours. This is where the entertainment material comes in handy, along with morale boosting luxuries like chocolate biscuits and real coffee bags.

This alternative procedure isn't always appropriate, of course; you may be too pressed for time if you have a tight schedule to meet. However, it should be considered seriously. In foul weather, your route may well need modifying, and now is the time to recheck your day's itinerary. Even if you don't intend to modify the route – and remember that Discretion is the better part of Experience – you'll often make up all your lost time over the day if you wait until the weather lifts, when you'll travel faster. The transistor radio, tuned into the weather forecast, can help you to make the decision here.

Finally, even if the foul weather looks set in for the day, or you've decided to pack up and go home, it's worth waiting a bit to see if a temporary respite will give you a chance at least to strike camp in relative comfort.

Camping in high winds

Camping in rain is easy enough if you follow the routine carefully. Camping in high winds, though, can be dangerous. If your tent is blown away the chance of exposure is great, particularly if it happens to be raining as well – and all too often it is.

If your camp site is fully exposed to winds of force seven or above (see pages 141–3), you may as well forget any attempt to pitch your tent. If there's no more sheltered site nearby, you can consider yourself to be in an emergency, and should resort to the sort of survival techniques explained in Chapter 8. Remember, though, you just shouldn't be in that situation.

If pitching the tent does seem feasible the first requirement is as sheltered a spot as you can find in the area. Level, dry ground definitely takes second place. Following the tent-pitching routine explained on pages 98–101 will make the job as easy as it can be, but try keeping a few rocks handy, to keep the tent down while spreading it out. In a group of two or more, someone can lie down on the canopy while pegs are put in. These pegs should be backed up with rocks or further pegs as a matter of course, however good the holding ground.

You'll also need extra guys, for which you can press into service your clothes line or walking rope but try to set these guys so that you don't have to cut the rope. The main danger, especially with ridge tents, is that the two ends of the tent wobble in different directions, the ridge pole comes apart and the fabric can rip under the strain. The extra guys, therefore, should lead from the back pole down the sides to the front of the tent, and from the front pole to the back in the same way.

Trying to cook inside a wind-battered tent is difficult. The fluttering walls create chaotic draughts from which it's virtually impossible to shield the stove flame. Naked flames inside a tent in these conditions are obviously highly dangerous anyway, which means that you can't use a candle either. So you may have to eat a cold meal in the dark.

To make matters worse the noise of flapping fabric will doom to failure any attempt at sleeping. This being the case, you may as well get up every hour or so to inspect pegs, guys and seams for signs of giving way. The slightest damage should be rectified at once, however difficult, or you will lose the tent.

Splitting seams are particularly dangerous. From personal experience, I can vouch for the strength of Micropore surgical tape plastered liberally over the beginnings of a tear, but a needle and thread are even better if it's humanly possible to use them without spilling too much blood.

Cooking in foul weather

Several references have already been made to the use of stoves inside tents. It's a potentially dangerous practice, and until you're well-used to living in a tent it's best avoided. Conditions are rarely such that cooking outside is impossible. It's just that it can be very uncomfortable. With tents featuring a bell-end porch, you can open this partially and cook in its shelter, and with Canadian-style tents, some compromise is feasible by placing the stove just outside the entrance. The cook can then squat in the entrance and stay dry. The entrance being at the leeward end of the tent means also that the kitchen will be sheltered from the wind.

The only danger here is that tent flaps, if not very neatly and firmly rolled and tied back out of the way, can flutter about, knock things over and even catch fire. It's a real danger; people do tend not to tie flaps back properly. I once saw two separate tents on one camp site burnt in this way.

If the weather's really bad, though, you may just have to move the kitchen into the tent. When a stove's belting out heat, while steam curls from your wet socks safety-pinned to the roof, and a candle flame is bathing the walls and your companions' faces in a warm yellow light, and the atmosphere is redolent with the smell of Oxo and wet wool, a weather-bound tent can seem quite cosy – until someone spills rice pudding on the groundsheet or sets fire to his sleeping bag.

Cosiness without the trouble can be enjoyed by following the system outlined below, but bear in mind that although it sounds easy it takes practice.

First, bring in a couple of large flat stones from outside and lay them on the groundsheet at the widest part of the tent. One provides a stable base for the stove and the other an insulated mat for hot pans. It is, of course, essential that you put nothing hot straight on to the groundsheet: even if you don't melt a hole in it you'll seriously weaken the fabric. When you're cooking in a bell-end porch, or at the tent entrance, you can rest the stove straight on the ground, but provide a mat for pans, as the ground will probably be wet and will soon get muddy. The bottoms of the pans will get dirty and this dirt will soon find its way on to sleeping bags and tent walls.

Now comes the difficult part. The cook must be allowed to do his job while the rest of the tent's occupants keep absolutely still and out of the way. Any movement will disturb the groundsheet and this movement will be transmitted to the stove and utensils. The stone mats help to minimize this, but do not eliminate it – a point which the cook should keep firm in mind.

Planning the meal and preparing the food for cooking is even more important than normal. Once the stove has been lit there should be no need for the cook to rummage about for items or even turn round for things behind him. It helps, in fact, if the remaining occupants of the tent are ready to follow the cook's orders, such as putting things down where he tells them to and holding utensils for him. The scene should really be reminiscent of an operating theatre, with the cook as surgeon.

Three further precautions should be taken. A problem pack should be positioned handy in case first aid is necessary, and all filling of stoves or changing of gas cartridges should be done outside the tent. I've never actually seen a tent blow up but I've heard of it happening. A more likely danger, yet one which is most frequently overlooked, is the fact that even if the stove is not near enough the tent fabric to scorch it, localized heat on the material weakens it very quickly until it's as brittle as rice-paper.

It's always supposed to be good practice to wash up immediately after a meal but if the pans need anything more than a quick wipe round and it's raining outside, forget it. Just stick them out in the rain. They'll get a good soaking which will make them easier to clean; and in any case it may stop raining later, enabling you to go and wash them without getting yourself wet.

Camping in difficult terrain

The problems mentioned so far in this chapter can occur more or less anywhere but the idea of camping in difficult terrain suggests that the expedition you're planning is an ambitious one. The very first rule, therefore, is to beware of taking on more than you can manage.

We're not talking here simply about wild country – there are many beautiful camping spots in remote corners of our moors and mountains that I wouldn't class as difficult terrain, but pitching your tent on a 1000m summit, or on a small ledge at the head of a gully that can only be reached by prolonged scrambling, or in the lee of a deep snowdrift, where you have to hack out a space first is strictly for the experienced, and you shouldn't contemplate such sites unless you're accompanied by an expert.

The first requirement will probably be a proper mountain tent. These tend to be rather lower in profile than the sort we've looked at so far. They're also heavier, being made of stronger fabric, and with more elaborate pole systems. Given the difficulty of pitching a tent with separate fly in the sort of weather likely to be encountered at altitude, they are also usually single skin or at least have the inner permanently attatched to the fly. Peg points are kept to a minimum since the ground is often too stony to drive pegs into, and to compensate for this, a wide flap, or valance, is fitted round the bottom. Stones or snow can be piled onto this to keep the tent down.

Preparing the site for the tent can be hard work particularly at the end of a difficult day's trek. First, a flat platform may have to be built. A compromise between levelling out the bumps and filling in the hollows is usually the best way. Pitching on really rocky ground calls for much scouring round to find suitable pebbles, earth and grass with which to fill the crevices.

If the ground is covered with snow, this should be cleared first, if possible, with your trowel and ice-axe. Don't pitch tents straight on top of snow if you can avoid it, since it will compact under the tent and form a sheet of cold, wet ice which hardly gives your ground insulation a chance. If the snow is too deep to clear then there should be enough for you to build a snow hole. Made properly these can be very cosy; I've spent several comfortable nights in them in Norway. You'll find instructions in Chapter 8.

Trying to push pegs into stony ground is a most frustrating business. You can sometimes drill the hole first with the spike on your clasp knife, or even with a thin cold chisel brought along specially for the job. If this doesn't work you can forget the pegs altogether and use loops of nylon cord threaded through the peg attachment points and tied on to the largest, heaviest rocks you can manhandle. If there are well-rooted trees or bushes handy you might belay to these.

The usual situation you will find is that pegs will go in about half-way. In this case there are two possibilities. Pegs holding out the guys can have rocks placed over the top of the guy just in front of the peg. This stops the guy riding up to the top of the peg and gives the peg itself something to pull against. Unless

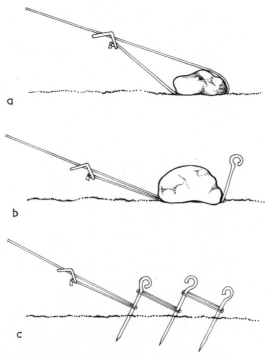

Fig. 25   Fixing guys in difficult ground: ensure that stones used in (a) and (b) have smooth rounded edges, to avoid chafing the guys; (c) is not safe unless at least half the peg is in the ground.

the rock has smooth, rounded edges it should be padded with moss or grass to protect the guy from chafe. Where there's no room to place a rock in front of the peg it can be backed up with a second, and even a third, peg driven in behind it and linked to it with a loop of cord. Figure 25 illustrates these two methods.

If your tent is fitted with a valance, place plenty of flat-bottomed stones all round it but take care that they don't touch the sides of the tent. If there's any wind and the tent starts fluttering it will chafe against the stones, very quickly wearing holes in the fabric.

The key to living in a tent pitched in difficult terrain is simplicity. Just getting to the site is probably going to be difficult, so you'll want to carry only the minimum of gear consistent with safety. That means leaving out the frills. Food, for example, can be reduced to basics. Soups and stews can form the basic diet; there's no need to distinguish between breakfast, lunch and supper. Utensils can be cut to one pan; most of the things in the ditty-bag can be left behind, and washing gear can be forgotten.

Gear will have to be very carefully checked and maintained since you'll be far from help should anything break, and preparation needs to be painstaking. Have you packed those nylon cord loops, for example? Do you have sufficient extra line to extend guys to the spot where they might best be secured? Have you double checked on the weather to ensure that you can retreat from this isolated position if necessary? Do you have a sufficient reserve of food supplies in case you are cut off? Could you cope if it was raining and blowing at the same time? Apart from being able to answer 'Yes' to all these questions, each member of the group should have complete mastery of all the skills outlined in this book.

It's probably true that nine times out of ten nothing will go wrong. And ninety-nine times out of a hundred you'll suffer only mild inconvenience from not knowing what to do or how to do it; it's the 1 per cent that's fatal though.

8 Staying alive

The safety factor

For the good expeditioner the safety factor is indissolubly linked with everything he does; it pervades his whole way of thinking, and all safety rules should quickly become second nature.

There are, of course, specific subjects connected with safety, such as first-aid or mountain-rescue techniques, but these require much more detailed study than a few pages can offer. If you want to specialize in first aid or learn more about mountain rescue you'll find details on who to contact in Chapter 10.

However, a good expeditioner is prepared for emergencies, and if you read this chapter you will know at least where to start if things go wrong.

First-aid kits

The problem pack described in Chapter 1 contains all you need for administering the sort of first aid you're competent to give unless you already hold a certificate from the St John's Ambulance Brigade, the St Andrew's Ambulance Association or the British Red Cross Society. However, on an extended expedition it would be sensible to take a larger kit which could contain the following items:

2 packets of paper tissue handkerchiefs (better than cotton wool for cleaning wounds)
3 compressed wound dressings – large, medium and small
1 crêpe bandage
1 gauze open-weave bandage
1 triangular bandage
1 tin assorted elastoplast patches

1 packet Scholl's 'Moleskin' for blisters

6 safety pins

1 tube Savlon (a detergent cleanser which is more use than antiseptic cream)

1 tube calamine cream (for sunburn, insect bites, etc)

1 packet soluble aspirin tablets (eg Codis)

1 packet Bisodol or Rennie's indigestion tablets (camp cooking, especially by novices, often leads to these being needed)

1 small pair of scissors

1 pair of tweezers

1 notepad and ball-point pen

All of these items can be obtained from chemists and can be packed into a suitable container, for example, a plastic food-box, and clearly marked. A list of contents taped to the inside of the lid will save people from rummaging through it for things that aren't there. I also include in mine – just in case it should be the first-aid expert in the group who's incapacitated – the *Spur Book of Outdoor First Aid*, an excellent little publication! As you can see, it's a basic kit with no sophisticated medical supplies.

Routine first aid

Very minor injuries – the cuts and scrapes that you normally lick and then ignore – need careful treatment in the field. Dirt finds expeditioners all too easily, and so you must take precautions against infection. Such injuries must be thoroughly cleansed with Savlon and purified drinking water. They should then be protected with a plain dressing. This cleansing is by far the most important part of first aid for minor injuries, and there's no substitute for it. Antiseptic creams applied to the surface of a wound will tend merely to seal in the germs.

Treatment for burns is the same whether they are minor or serious. The affected area should be immersed in cold water immediately, and kept there for at least ten minutes; any shorter time is useless. This lowers skin temperature, relieves pain, and minimizes the blistering which leads to subsequent scarring. The burn can then be protected with a dry, non-fluffy dressing. On no account should you burst any blisters that do form.

A serious burn will cause severe shock which may even immobilize the patient and will lead to loss of much body fluid which must be replaced by giving the patient half a cup of water every ten minutes, assuming he's conscious, of course. Any burn which removes more than a square centimetre of skin requires qualified medical attention so treat it as an emergency and abandon your expedition, at least until you've sought a doctor's advice.

Foot blisters can be totally incapacitating so perhaps they should be regarded as at least potentially serious. Due care, however, will minimize the risk so effectively that they ought really to be considered, like sunburn, as a self-inflicted injury. Clean, dry socks on clean feet are the first line of defence, assuming that your boots fit well. Chapter 1 deals with these points at length.

If a hot spot starts to develop try changing your socks from one foot to another. The effect is largely psychological but seems to work. Blisters that still insist on forming should be covered with 'Moleskin' or, failing that, a strip of Micropore tape folded so that sticky sides are together and secured in place with another piece of the same. Ordinary Elastoplast does not work for this purpose. The area *around* the blister can be slightly padded with tissues to keep pressure off the spot, but watch that the added pressure under the tissue doesn't create problems of its own.

Don't burst blisters even though some authorities say you can. In my experience, people who do this tend to regret it, if only because they fail to sterilize the needle properly. Blisters that burst of their own accord, which they will do only if you're stupid enough to ignore them once they have formed, should be carefully cleaned after removing all loose skin with scissors and covered with a dressing, as for burns. If you can expose them to the air for a while to dry out first this will help.

Finally, in connection with routine first aid, we must consider the use of pain killers. Caution should be exercised in treatment even of mild head and stomach-aches. They could be symptoms of something more serious, which drugs might conceal until it's too late. You then have a real emergency on your hands. I once treated an expeditioner for indigestion, only to discover that he had a history of grumbling appendix which he'd concealed from me. Now all students in my group have to complete a form, to be signed by parents, giving details of any such ailment. It's worth checking the medical history of your companions.

Accident procedure

With care and attention to the content of this book, you shouldn't ever experience anything approaching a real emergency in which a member of your party is seriously injured. However, there's always the possibility that you'll come across someone who is, and accidents can happen, even on the best-planned expeditions.

Medical treatment of serious injuries is obviosuly best left to experts, but initial life-saving first aid is often necessary before the experts can be brought in. The following procedure will give the casualty the best chance of survival in the hands of his unskilled companions.

1 Whatever the injury or position of the casualty, check to see that he's breathing freely. In many accidents breathing is obstructed by the casualty choking on vomit, loose teeth, or even his tongue. Scoop out any debris with your fingers, hold his jaw closed and tilt his head back as far as possible to keep the air passages clear. In moving the patient like this, you have to accept the principle of the calculated risk; you may aggravate his injuries but if you don't do it you may well let him die.

If the casualty is still not breathing, give mouth-to-nose resuscitation. The easiest way to do this is to hold the jaw shut with one hand which can also push the head back. Place your mouth over the casualty's nose, and turn your head slightly so that your cheek blocks off his mouth. In mouth-to-mouth

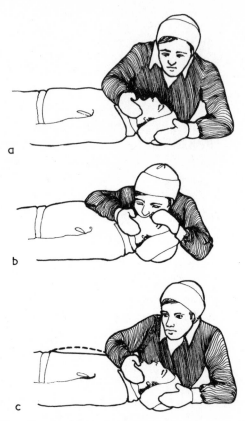

Fig. 26 Artificial resuscitation – mouth-to-nose method: (a) tilt head back and close mouth; (b) inflate chest by blowing through nose; (c) check that chest deflates. If nose is injured, give resuscitation via mouth but check that tongue does not obstruct airway.

resuscitation, which isn't quite so satisfactory but is sometimes necessary when the nose is damaged, you block off the nostrils with your other cheek. Now breathe out firmly, check that the chest wall rises and let it fall at its own pace; then repeat. Half-a-dozen quick breaths should be followed by steady breathing at about ten cycles to the minute.

The old-fashioned method of resuscitation, in which you lay the patient on his front and lean on his back, is obviously potentially dangerous. Should the casualty be suffering internal injuries you will merely aggravate them. In any case, it's much less efficient than the mouth-to-mouth method.

Accidents in wild country rarely result in the casualty's breathing being fully stopped. All the same, if you get the chance to learn and practise artificial resuscitation, take it. One day someone might just be glad you did.

2 Before manhandling the casualty any further, examine him as carefully as possible to determine the nature of the injuries. The most dangerous, of course, is a broken back. Even if the casualty isn't paralysed yet, inexpert handling may well finish him off. If you simply have to move him to avoid further injury, for example from a rock-fall, keep the back absolutely rigid in its original position. You need at least four helpers, perferably more, and I confess I quake at the thought of attempting it.

If you can, make a written note of all injuries, describing what you see even if you can't actually diagnose it. This will be of great help to doctors later on. Apart from obvious injuries like wounds, limbs held unnaturally, swollen joints and tenderness in any spot indicate broken bones. Unequally dilated pupils, blood from the ears and snoring, with unconsciousness, suggest a fractured skull. Paleness, shivering while sweating and abnormal thirst – which you shouldn't allow the patient to quench just yet – are symptoms of severe shock. It's also wise to consider the possibility of internal injuries. If they're causing any internal bleeding, this may be indicated by a quickening of the pulse.

The easiest place in which to feel the pulse is in the patient's neck. A finger laid across either side of his throat will make contact with his carotid artery. Alternatively, with practice, you can find the pulse point in the wrist. Don't use your thumb, which has its own pulse, to feel that of your patient.

3 Any serious bleeding must be stopped as soon as possible. This much you can do while examining the casualty, or even while someone else is giving artificial resuscitation. The method is simply to apply a pad of material to the wound and bandage firmly. Don't try to tidy up the wound, don't remove the bandage if it doesn't appear to work – just put another one on top – and don't, ever, use a tourniquet. Check very carefully, too, beneath the casualty and under clothing which may be concealing the blood from unsuspected wounds. Don't panic: $\frac{1}{2}$ litre of blood spreads a long way but its loss isn't too serious. Loss of more than $\frac{1}{2}$ litre is; so stop it fast.

4 Immobilize broken limbs if necessary. You shouldn't try to splint them unless you're going to attempt moving the patient. Just support them with improvised padding in their original position and make the patient as comfortable as possible. If you do have to move the patient and therefore need to splint broken

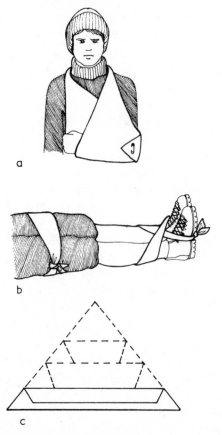

Fig. 27   Using triangular bandages: (a) an arm sling – position knot on side opposite injury; (b) securing legs and feet with padding between them. Leave boots on; (c) folding bandage for use as splint.

limbs you can tie arms across the chest and legs to each other, having padded all hollows beforehand.

If the patient is unconscious and his injuries don't make it absolutely impossible to move him, then, accepting again the calculated risk, he should be placed in the recovery position with his head slightly downhill if possible. Figure 28 illustrates it. The patient lies on his front, one leg bent and with one arm upwards. His head is turned to one side and rests facing the hand of the raised arm. This is the most stable position in which to lie, and ensures that when he comes to, he will not further injure himself with uncontrolled movement, or choke if he vomits – as he may well do. Nor will he swallow his tongue or otherwise obstruct his breathing while unconscious.

Fig. 28   Recovery position: head should preferably point slightly down hill.

5 Make the patient comfortable and relieve pain, if possible. It may be tempting to give pain killers, but if there's any suspicion of internal injuries or any chance of the casualty reaching an operating table within the next eight hours, don't. The basic rule is not to administer anything by mouth. The only exceptions are with conscious burnt patients (or conscious poisoned ones) as explained on page 124, and with cases of exhaustion-exposure, for which see below.

Now is the time to wrap the patient up in a space blanket or bivvy bag, and to pitch the tent over him if you're carrying one or provide other shelter from the elements for both of you. Look after yourself as well; you will have been working hard, under stress and in difficult conditions. You've got to remain in control of the situation for a while yet until help is fetched, so make yourself comfortable, keep calm and try to reassure your patient as much as possible.

As far as first aid is concerned, there's little else you can do. The business of fetching help is a problem on its own, which we'll look at later. Meanwhile, you can do more harm than good by 'over-treating' the patient. However, do keep checking on his condition, and be on the alert for any deterioration while you're awaiting help. And bear in mind that this five-point casualty code is a useful instant response, but it does not constitute a course in first aid. It's a subject worth studying further.

Exhaustion-exposure

Exhaustion-exposure is what causes hypothermia. In theory, it shouldn't occur if you follow the advice given in previous chapters of this book, and in particular the sections on clothing, sheltering and eating on the trail. However, it *can* happen to anyone, however well prepared they think they are; it frequently does, and it's a killer.

What happens is that your inner body-temperature drops – and it only has to drop a little – whereupon your vital organs cease to function. And it can take as little as an hour from the first signs until death. Causes can include inadequate clothing to protect against heat loss in foul weather, insufficient food intake to fuel replacement heat, and physical tiredness preventing you from exercising hard enough to generate it. Just one of these is enough to start a downward spiral, starting with excessive cooling of your skin and culminating, as blood vessels close down and body tissue becomes contaminated by toxins which your blood normally flushes away, with the poisoning of your brain.

You're most at risk when everything else is going wrong. Imagine, for example, that you've lost your way temporarily; that you're faced as a result with a longer walk back to base than you expected; that the weather has deteriorated and it's getting towards dusk; and water has found its way inside your boots, giving you cold, wet feet. At this point, morale is low and, at the very time when you should be taking extra care of yourself, you tend to let the routine slide. At times like this, remember Resolution.

The symptoms of hypothermia are difficult to detect and can occur in any order and at any stage of its development. Perhaps the most realistic method of diagnosing it is the one taught by the Army in its expedition training manual; namely, take action if any two of the following symptoms appear, either together or one after the other:

Complaints of cold, tiredness and cramp
Lethargy – a 'don't care any more' attitude
Lack of understanding of simple questions and directions
Slurring of speech
Frequent stumbling or lack of co-ordination
Abnormality of vision
Unusual behaviour, such as violent activity from normally quiet people, or silence from the normally talkative
Collapse and coma

The treatment is simple. Stop. Find or build shelter. Dress the casualty in any extra clothing available and – most important this – surround him with a waterproof, windproof layer. The bivvy bag or space blanket is ideal. If possible, place a fit person inside the bag with him. If you have a sleeping bag, place him in that before putting him in the bivvy bag. And if you have a tent, pitch it and fill it up with people.

The idea is to prevent any further heat loss by adding to the insulation and preventing evaporation. Clothing that is already damp will conduct heat away from the body very quickly if exposed to the wind, but will provide perfectly good insulation if protected by that impermeable layer and by placing the casualty in shelter. Experts are still debating this, but I feel that soaking-wet clothes are best removed if there is something drier to replace them with.

Next brew up a warm drink for the casualty, assuming that he's conscious and that he's not actually feeling sick. The digestive organs are some of the first to shut down as hypothermia develops, so use some caution here. If humanly possible, though, get him to take some easily digested, high calorie food. This is where the Complan in your emergency rations is useful.

This food will fuel the casualty's body and give him a chance to start generating more heat. The process can be helped by warming the atmosphere around him – hence the fit person in the bivvy bag with him and the over-crowding of the tent. Do not, however, under *any* circumstances, apply local heat like an improvised hot water bottle, or by rubbing his skin in an attempt to warm it. You will merely draw vital warm blood from the internal organs to the cold, deoxygenated, toxin-laden surface tissue, from which it will return to the core even cooler and more contaminated.

Remember also one further point. If one member of the party is suffering from exhaustion-exposure, the chances are that the rest of the group is nearing the brink. Everyone should take advantage of the hot brew, the food and the shelter. In any case, there's no question of continuing your trek, even if your patient appears to be improving. You're going to be there some time before you're rescued, so you may as well make yourself comfortable.

Bivouacking

If you're stuck in wild country waiting for help and you have no tent you'll need to improvise shelter. There are three possibilities, apart from the impractical bowers of green branches and convenient fallen tree-trunks so beloved of books on survival.

The first, and most obvious, is to use existing artificial shelter – a barn, a derelict house, or even the plastic bags and corrugated iron that seem to litter our countryside these days. If shelter has to be built from local materials its exact style will obviously depend on what's available, but the following general guide-lines may be useful.

Keep it as small and low as possible to conserve heat. If you utilize or build a stone wall, ensure that all chinks which might otherwise let in the wind are filled with moss, mud or grass. Make the entrance as small as you can and once you're inside block it up completely if you can. Cover the ground with as much dry material as possible – heather, bracken, hay bales, coiled rope – anything that will insulate you from the cold earth.

Since the shelter won't show up like a space blanket or a tent, set out a large signal outside. One of the best materials to hand is your roll of toilet tissue, particularly if you buy a bright pink one. Simply unroll it and weight it down with stones. If it's raining it will soon stick to the ground anyway.

The second possibility, in snow conditions, is a snow-hole. Old, firm snow is needed. Most drifts consist of layers of hard and soft snow so position your snow-hole so that floor and ceiling coincide with two layers. Start by hacking out a small tunnel with your ice-axe. Once it's long enough for you to crawl in, enlarge the inside. There should be a broad shelf above the level of the entrance, on which you can sit; and because there will be some melting of the walls and roof with your body heat, you should cut a small trench round the edge of this shelf. See Figure 29.

In level snow you can improvise a little igloo with large snowballs. Don't attempt to build a traditional dome-shaped one; a pyramid is much easier. Snow that's too hard to roll into balls can be hacked up in square blocks and stood on edge. In these conditions, it's probably easier to use a space blanket or bivvy sheet as the roof.

Whatever sort of snow-hole you construct make sure you have a snowball ready to block the entrance, and that you have an air hole to the surface. Keep this air hole clear with the shaft of your ice-axe. If you can find a longer stick, so much the

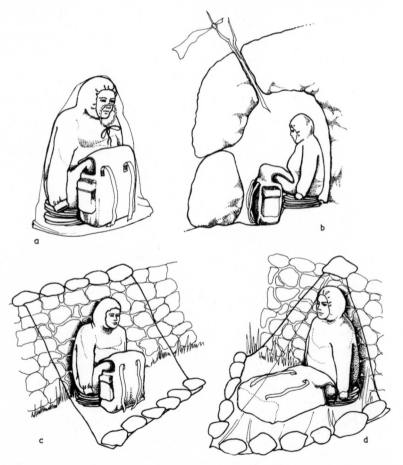

Fig. 29   Bivouacs: (a) sitting inside plastic bivvy bag with hole cut for face; (b) snow hole with signal projecting from ventilation hole; (c) lean-to bivouac made from plastic sheet; (d) wedge bivouac, offering better shelter.

better. You can tie an improvised flag to the end and poke this through to the surface. Waggling the stick will not only keep the air hole clear but will draw attention to your whereabouts.

The third possibility is a tent improvised from a bivvy bag or sheet. In the case of the bag, there's nothing to be done but crawl into it. With the sheet, however, it's best to construct some kind of lean-to. Two possibilities appear in Figure 29. In the first, a 3m length of nylon cord is fixed to the top of a wall and led down to the ground where it's secured with a peg. The bivvy sheet is then draped over this diagonally so that one corner may be secured with a heavy stone on top of the wall and its opposite reaches the ground by the peg. The sides can then be stretched out and weighted down so that an enclosed wedge-shaped tent is formed, with the wall forming the back. Having squeezed between the wall and the edge of the sheet, you'll find yourself well protected from the elements with just enough room to sit well huddled up. The second version is more roomy, and will let two of you find shelter, but is open at the ends.

Whatever your form of shelter, there are other precautions you must take. Empty your rucksack, put on all your reserve clothing and place your feet in the sack, boots and all, and, of course, wrap yourself up in a space blanket, if you have one. You can minimize heat loss further by taking your arms out of your cagoule and zipping it up round you, with your arms inside the main body of your garment. Don't forget that some insulation is needed from the ground where you sit; also, assuming you're not alone, huddle together for warmth.

Fetching help

The Mountain-rescue authorities do suggest that in the event of an emergency you should make an effort to get back to civilization yourself, and that the rescue team should only be called out as a last resort. Obviously the teams need to be able to concentrate on the genuinely immobile casualties, not merely on people who feel the need for a bit of moral support on their way home.

However, if you're at all inexperienced and uncertain of

what to do, trying to get an injured or unfit person out of wild
country will probably just make matters worse. Improvising a
stretcher isn't as easy as it sounds, and carrying it over rough
terrain is a skilled exercise. Even sharing out a disabled
companion's pack between the rest of you can prove too much
of an extra burden. Weather conditions, too, may force you to
find shelter and stay put rather than risk exhaustion-exposure
trying to help yourself. Remember that a party which decides
to bivvy down and sit out a storm, or wait until daylight
because it's lost and benighted, is not necessarily in trouble.
It's just being sensible.

This same sense of caution should apply when you're
sending members of the party for help. On the whole, you're
safer staying put until help arrives, but don't feel, just because
you've been benighted, that you have to wait for help even
when morning arrives with better weather and finds you fit. In
this case, get up and go to a telephone as quickly as possible.

However, if you're in the situation where you can't move out
on your own – where you have an immobile casualty, for
example, and prompt medical attention is needed if the
casualty is not to die – two of you will have to fetch help. With
smaller parties, the problem of leaving the casualty unattended
raises its head. If at all possible, don't. And if at all possible,
don't let one person go for help alone; the risks are obvious.
Now you see why there should really be at least four of you.

With fetching help, as with everything, you can adopt a set
routine. First, check the map carefully to establish your exact
position, and then plan the fastest safe route out that is
possible. Your route card should already contain details of
possible escape routes and locations of phones and rescue
posts. Now write down the details of the emergency as follows:

1 The nature of the emergency (type of accident, with
   details of injuries, exhaustion-exposure, etc.)
2 The number of casualties, and others still at location
3 The location, with a description of the area as well as a
   grid reference
4 The time of the accident

5 The equipment available at the location and brief details of help already given

Having it on paper will help you to remember everything when you arrive, exhausted probably, at the phone. On dialling 999 and calling for the police or the rescue service, you'll be asked your name and probably told to stand by the phone. Do just that. Even if you're not fit enough to go back out with the rescue team to lead them to your party, they'll want to talk to you to get further details.

If you're going to fetch help you must ensure that you yourself are adequately equipped to survive the prevailing conditions; given this need, travel as light as possible. Hurry, but don't run. Pace yourself carefully and you'll get there more quickly in the end.

Those left behind to wait for rescue will find time dragging, so don't give them any chance to be disappointed or worried by suggesting that you'll be back in an impossibily short time. If you can calculate the time it will take to reach the phone or the mountain-rescue post to which you're heading double that, double it again, and you'll have some idea of when they might begin to expect help to arrive. However, weather conditions and terrain will have a significant effect on this schedule, so err on the long side – and your friends may be in for a pleasant surprise when help arrives before they expect it.

If you're one of those left behind you must make a deliberate effort to keep morale up. The time-honoured tricks of playing word games and so on do work. Any flags and signs you're proposing to put out should be positioned in good time, but don't waste your torch battery or your breath signalling for help when there can't possibly be anyone around to notice. This doesn't mean you shouldn't try at all. Giving the Alpine distress signal can be your first step towards finding help. It's described in Chapter 1 (see page 18).

Helicopters

RAF helicopters are being increasingly used in conjunction with civilian rescue organizations and, being the professionals they are, the crews turn out in the most impossible conditions. However, they should not be called on to provide chauffeured transport home for people who are just feeling fed up: you have no right to demand their assistance.

Should a helicopter be called out for you the best way you can help it is to get onto open ground where it can approach easily, make yourself conspicuous so that the crew can see you, and keep still. It's worth pointing out that the pilot can't see you when he's hovering overhead, and relies on the winch-man for guidance. It makes life very difficult for them if you keep moving about.

Don't just wave at helicopters if you need help. Stand with your arms stretched up and out, like a letter Y. If all is well and you need no help the recognized signal is supposed to be one arm raised vertically with fist clenched.

Afterwards

When it's all over, do write and thank the people who risked their lives for you. Even better, make a donation to the mountain-rescue team funds. In addition, you'll naturally have some very hard thinking to do. What went wrong? Why? Was it your fault? The answer to the last question, though it may seem unfair, is probably 'Yes'.

9 Weather forecasting

The point of it

One of the great rewards of expeditioning is learning to live with the elements. It's possible if you have good equipment and know how to use it, to plod on and survive. It's much more satisfying, though, to exploit the weather, rather as sailors do. Choosing a route where the wind is at your back or the clouds are shrouding some other mountain or sitting in your tent watching the rain fall, having chosen a camp site you could reach before the bad weather caught up with you, creates a delicious feeling of smugness as well as comfort.

Before going on an expedition, you will, of course, have obtained a weather forecast. These are obtainable through the radio and television. However, these are of necessity rather generalized, covering wide areas and taking little account of local variations. A forecast for a specific area is best obtained by ringing up the meteorological office nearest to it. You can find the number in the front of the telephone directory for the area. This method has the advantage that you can leave it until the very last minute when you're in the area; and so you get the very latest, updated version.

Unfortunately, though, weather has a habit of changing rapidly – and, locally at least, not always in accordance with the forecast – so the experienced expeditioner tends to be rather preoccupied with predicting the weather in the field. To do this with any degree of accuracy you need more than a few rules of thumb like 'high wispy clouds mean wind' or 'Red sky at night: shepherd's delight'. You need an intelligent understanding of wind and cloud movement, and of the underlying weather patterns which cause them.

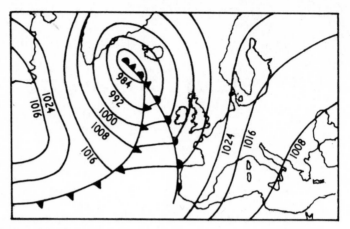

Fig. 30 Weather map: this is typical of newspaper weather maps. The numbers refer to pressure in millibars.

Frontal systems

Figure 30 is a picture of a frontal system. Weather charts like this can be found in the newspapers. The following should make it easier to understand them.

Weather changes are caused by variations in air pressure from one area to another, and these are measured by the *barometer*. The unit of measurement is a *millibar*. If, at a given time, you join up all the points on the map where the air pressure is the same you get a series of lines which look like contours and are called *isobars*.

If you think of these as contours, they give a very clear picture of where the areas of high and low pressure are. The distance apart of the isobars illustrates the *pressure gradient*; a steep gradient gives rise to strong winds and a gentle one to lighter breezes. The areas of low pressure are called *depressions* or *lows* and those of high pressure are *anticyclones* or *highs*.

Along with depressions we get phenomena known as *fronts* where a cold air-stream, usually from the north-east, meets a warm one, usually coming from the south-west. When the two air-streams meet the warm air tends to rise above the cold and this causes the drop in pressure. The cold air moves in to fill the gap, spiralling towards the centre of the depression at an angle of about 15° to the isobars. Thus are created the winds. Figure 31 shows the cross section of such a front.

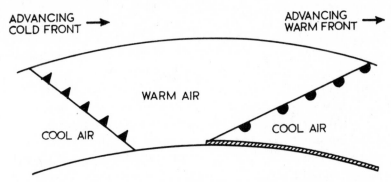

ADVANCING COLD FRONT →

ADVANCING WARM FRONT →

WARM AIR

COOL AIR

COOL AIR

Fig. 31   Sectional view of a frontal system: note that the cold front is 'steeper' than the warm one, producing more violent weather changes.

As the depression moves eastwards the wedge of warm air moves with it. The leading edge is called a *warm front* simply because it's the front edge of the warm air mass. As it passes we're overtaken by the *cold front* – the front edge of the cold air following the wedge. Eventually, the cold air will slide right under the wedge of warm air to form a continuous layer of cold air at ground level with a warm air layer on top. This is called an *occluded front* and is usually a sign that the depression – and the bad weather associated with it – is breaking up.

On the weather charts, the cold front is indicated by black triangles along a line representing its advancing edge; and the symbol for a warm front is a similar line bearing half circles. An occluded front is marked by alternate semi-circles and triangles. If you go back and study Figure 30 more closely now it should begin to make sense.

Winds

In the field you can actually see wind coming by watching the clouds, and feel it with the change of wind direction. The wind high up in the sky will start spiralling in towards the centre of a depression before you feel it at ground level, so watch the way the clouds are moving. As a general rule, if you stand with your back to the wind the worst of the weather will be to your left: worth bearing in mind when you're deciding which way to walk!

The strength of the wind will indicate the severity of the depression, but your main concern will be with its potential as an exposure hazard. The stronger the wind, the greater its chill factor. Forecasts intended for shipping use the *Beaufort Scale*. In the field wind speed is most easily estimated by this means so the scale is reproduced below, with equivalent wind speeds in miles per hour, and some comments on the sort of conditions you might expect for any given wind strength.

The Beaufort Scale

Force	Wind speed in mph	Comments
0	Under 1	Calm. Smoke rises vertically. Match flame steady.
1	1–3	Smoke drifts. Flame flickers.
2	4–7	Light wind can be felt on face. Leaves and grass tussocks rustle.
3	8–12	Twigs on trees move. Long grass begins to wave. Camping stoves need wind shields.
4	13–18	Moderate breeze. Dust blown about. Smaller branches swayed. Some care needed in pitching tents.
5	19–24	Begins to feel chilly. Small trees sway. Short grass ripples. Pitching tents begins to be tricky.
6	25–31	Uncomfortable to walk against. Telephone wires hum. Large branches sway. The strongest wind in which it's practicable to pitch tents with separate fly.

7	32–38	Near gale. Large trees sway. Walking against wind difficult. Danger of being blown off balance on exposed ridges. Tents need extra guying.
8	39–46	Gale. Tree branches fall. tents need even more extra guying and pegs reinforcing.
9	47–54	Some structural damage to houses, so tents not very safe either.
10	55–63	Large trees uprooted. Tents will probably disintegrate.
11	64–72	Severe storm. You've got problems.
12	73 upwards	Hurricane. You're past caring about your problems.

Think carefully about these comments. Wild country can be very difficult to traverse in high winds, and camping can be fraught with risk. Winds of force 8 and above don't happen very often below about 600m, and you wouldn't entertain going out in them if you could avoid it. Be warned that people who talk glibly about having camped in gales are usually thinking of ground-level winds around force 6.

You can think of the exposure hazard in terms of *wind-chill*. If the air temperature in a force 3 breeze is around 10°C, it will feel 5° colder. If the wind speed increases to force 5, the equivalent temperature drops to freezing, and in a force 7 near-gale, it reaches down to −5°C. In addition, there's something called the *lapse rate*. As you climb in mountainous terrain the air temperature drops by about 3°C per 300m. To look at an example, if the temperature at sea level is a sunny 18°C, then on the top of Snowdon with the wind blowing a steady force 4 it will be just about freezing. These conditions can occur even in high summer, so never be tempted to leave your reserve warm wear behind because the weather seems warm when you set off.

Clouds in a frontal system

At ground level the wind in wild country tends to be deflected from its true course. Mountains, valleys and ridges all tend to obstruct it and funnel it in misleading directions so it's the clouds that give you a true indication of the weather, not only by the way in which they're moving, but by their shape as well.

The highest type of cloud is *cirrus*, forming sometimes as much as 13km up. It heralds a change of weather, appearing for example some twelve to eighteen hours ahead of an advancing warm front or trailing behind a passing cold one. It appears as white, wispy patches, bands or tufted streaks which are sometimes called 'mares tails'.

A development of this is *cirrostratus* which looks like a thin white veil. In quantity it indicates a break up in the weather. As a warm front approaches the cloud thickens and becomes *altostratus* which looks like a sheet of satin. The sun or moon may be visible through it at first. This is sometimes called a 'watery sun'. The first intermittent drops of rain may start falling from this cloud eight to fourteen hours after the first approach of cirrostratus. The wind will probably be backing (moving anticlockwise) during this time, towards the south.

With the continuing approach of the front the cloud will get thicker and lower till it becomes *stratocumulus*, a thick grey sheet with a base consisting of billows and rolls. It usually forms anywhere between 500 and 3000m, and is one of the two sorts of cloud you're likely to walk into on the mountains. The other sort is *stratus*, a very low, flat grey sheet forming below the main cloud base. By the time this appears rain will probably be continuous. When it thickens to a shapeless billowing mass, the top of which, incidentally, may be very high, it's called *nimbus*. It usually produces very heavy rain.

As the warm front passes the heavier rain gives way to lighter rain or drizzle. In fact, it may, especially in summer, stop altogether. The wind generally veers (moves clockwise) and decreases in strength. In summer the cloud base will probably lift – except occasionally in western parts of the country, especially if the wedge of air behind the warm front is part of a very warm, moist, south-westerly airflow. In this case you can expect hill and coastal fog.

Again in summer, especially inland and to the east of high ground, the cloud in this warm sector can break to give sunny intervals, but don't get too optimistic; the weather's going to get worse again! The onset of the cold front is usually accompanied by a further veering of the wind, thickening cloud and more rain. As the front passes the air temperature will fall and the cloud will begin to break up to form strato-cumulus and *cumulus* – the cloud that looks like bunches of cotton wool.

If this breaks up into small fleecy lumps in a blue sky you can expect them to disperse at sunset. They are an indication of fair weather, heralding the presence of an anticyclone with light winds. Not that you can relax, even now. There's a good chance of early morning mist in summer and frost from autumn through to spring. And more usually, the cumulus following a cold front will grow into *cumulonimbus* when the clouds, which will be large with dark flat bases, develop anvil-shaped tops and produce very heavy showers, possibly of hail. By now, the wind will be blowing north-easterly to northerly.

In occluded fronts the weather passes directly from the pre-warm-front rain to the cooler, showery air-stream without the break in between. The wind shift is even more marked.

This may all seem a little technical, but it's worth taking the trouble to understand because by far the greater part of our weather is caused by these frontal systems. Watching it change is fascinating when you know what's going to happen next, but such knowledge also enables you to make realistic plans on how to live with the weather, rather than having to grit your teeth and hope for the best.

Thunderstorms

Thunderstorms are phenomena that, with experience, you learn to predict. In theory, your hair, particularly on arms, will tend to stand on end. Any sizeable metal objects you're carrying, such as pack frame or ice-axe, will make your fingers tingle when you touch them. They may even buzz audibly. In practice, you'll get an earlier warning if you let the birds do the predicting. They tend to disappear in good time.

There's no real danger that you'll be struck by lightning unless the storm is right on top of you and you're standing near a good conductor. When taking shelter, therefore, keep away from trees, fences, sharp ridges and summits, and avoid standing up in the midlde of flat open ground, where you yourself might become a conductor. Don't take shelter in a cave or under an overhang either; lightning has a habit of striking the lip of rock above such features. That doesn't leave much choice, but if you sit behind a *low* wind-break or in a slight open hollow until the storm has passed on a little you should be safe enough. Counting the seconds between the flashes and the thunder and dividing by three will give your approximate distance from the storm in kilometres.

Fog

To conclude this chapter, we should take a look at one of the most common, yet unpredictable, phenomena you're likely to meet: fog. It may be that you're simply high enough up to be caught in the clouds, or that the moisture in air that cools and sinks to the ground condenses to form the low-lying mist that often fills the valleys in the early morning. This happens particularly when the sky is clear during the night. The most persistent form, though – known as 'clag' to hardened expeditioners – occurs in fairly calm conditions when warm air comes into contact with cold ground. A moist, south-westerly wind over wet, boggy or high moorland is a sure recipe, particularly in winter when the ground temperature is low.

Early morning mist is soon dissipated as the day warms up and if your camp site is well chosen you will at least be near the top of the layer if not above it altogether. If you wake up to a bright mist which seems to glow with diffused sunlight you can prospect a little up any slopes above the camp site to see if it shows signs of thinning. If it does, then you're probably safe to set out on your trek, but be meticulous about your navigation, and be prepared to think again if it doesn't soon disperse.

You might think that you'd know well enough when you're heading into cloud but it has a habit of rolling in around the corner suddenly without warning. It can then disappear just as quickly or thicken until you feel as though you're eating it. Treat it seriously, simply because it is so unpredictable. Likewise, 'clag' calls for care. You're unlikely to walk out of it for some time, and walking through it will slow you down.

If there's any chance of fog or mist – we may regard the first as merely a thicker form of the second – then keep a sharp watch on the horizon. If it starts to blur in any way, or if the air turns chilly and you suddenly find you can look straight at the sun, expect fog, and think about the advice given on pages 64–7.

Fixing your position while you can still see the landmarks is particularly important; you may have very little time before visibility deteriorates. And when it does, don't assume that it will improve in a hurry.

In fact, don't assume anything with regard to the weather. There are so many variations and local influences that you must always be prepared for the unexpected.

10 Opportunities

Clubs

The advantages of belonging to a club are several. Most obvious is the social aspect; you meet other people with similar interests. Most clubs run regular social meetings at which experiences are recounted and ideas swapped. In this way, you pick up a great deal of knowledge and expertise.

In addition, many clubs have numerous facilities of which you can take advantage. Most of the larger equipment retailers offer special discount terms to clubs, often in the region of 20 per cent for bulk orders. By purchasing your gear through the club you can make quite a saving. Then there are sometimes pools of equipment belonging to the club from which you can borrow; and you'll find at least some of the other members quite willing to lend you items of their own. This all enables you to test and assess equipment for yourself before laying out money. In these respects it's worth considering the idea of starting up your own club if you can't find one to suit.

Established clubs will also have experience of likely expeditioning areas; they can advise on camp sites, official and unofficial, which are on the most interesting routes, and can even help with getting you there, perhaps on a transport-sharing basis. Once in the area, you may be able to benefit from a club hut: many clubs have simple hostels or bunk houses in attractive and conveniently situated wild country.

One final advantage, less obvious but maybe in the long run most important, is the fact that the club you join will probably be affiliated to some national organization like the British Mountaineering Council, which has an influential voice in matters of deciding how the public should be served by our available countryside.

If you have difficulty finding a local club, write to the BMC.

The address is in Appendix 1. The monthly magazine, *Climber and Rambler*, which is the official journal of the BMC also publishes a list of clubs and their activities in each issue.

Courses and training

The sort of training you receive in a local club will probably be informal and relaxed. If you want something more concentrated you could seek professional instruction at an outdoor pursuits centre. The best known of these are Glemore Lodge in Aviemore, Scotland, and Plas Y Brenin in North Wales, both, indirectly, government sponsored. The Outward Bound Trust also runs mountain schools in various parts of the country. In addition, there are numerous privately run centres which can offer instruction, with equipment and qualified leadership provided.

If you're still at school you may find that outdoor pursuits are part of the curriculum, and even if they're not most local education authorities now sponsor such activities. The school secretary can put you in touch with the authority's youth officer or physical education adviser who can give you details.

Through almost any of these organizations you can take courses leading to official qualifications such as the Mountain Leadership Certificate or the Duke of Edinburgh's Award (expediton section). Or you can just go along to learn a little, without trying to bag certificates.

Apart from such centres, organizations like the Scout and Guide Associations and indeed the Duke of Edinburgh's Award Scheme, can offer opportunities for training in expeditioning. In the field of first aid, the British Red Cross Society, the St John's Ambulance Brigade and, in Scotland, the St Andrew's Ambulance Association, run local classes in all areas. For information on Scouts, Guides or the Duke of Edinburgh's Award Scheme, you can write direct to their head offices, as an alternative to making local inquiries, but communications to the first-aid organizations should be addressed to the local detachment whose address you'll find in the telephone directory.

Information services

The National Trust owns large tracts of land as well as monuments and buildings of interest. Local advice can be given by the wardens in charge of each area whose names and addresses you can get from the head office or in some cases from the telephone directory. It's worth remembering though, that The National Trust, as a matter of firm policy, prohibits 'indiscriminate' camping on its land – and does seem to regard as such all privately organized lightweight camping.

More helpful, from the point of view of finding camp sites, is the Forestry Commission which can also recommend routes through its land and has set up special scenic and nature trails for public use.

Details regarding the national parks and long-distance footpaths are most conveniently obtained from the Countryside Commission. However, if you're planning a visit to a national park with a large group of young people (a school party or youth club, say) you'll be given a great deal of practical help by the youth liaison officer of that park's committee. Write to him direct once you've obtained the current address from the Countryside Commission. You'll find a list of the national parks and the long-distance footpaths at the end of Appendix 1.

Climber and Rambler, already mentioned, and its sister magazine, *The Great Outdoors*, cover the whole spectrum of expeditioning, from technical rock-climbing, through Himalayan peak-conquering, to camping club rallies. They also contain directories of equipment retailers, as well as the club lists referred to earlier. Through their advertisements you can often find bargains in second-hand gear, and of course you can learn about what equipment is available in general. You'll also find advertised details of training courses and outdoor pursuits centres, while the magazine articles themselves are informative and helpful. Manufacturers' catalogues are also full of useful information – but bear in mind that they are trying to sell you the equipment, so think carefully about whether it's really what you want.

As a precautionary measure you should obtain and read

Mountain and Cave Rescue, the handbook of the Mountain Rescue Committee. Apart from listing all the mountain-rescue teams operating in this country and the locations of mountain rescue posts, it contains much useful summarized information on survival and self-help. You can get it from the secretary of the MRC. Equally useful and concise is the BMC booklet, *Safety on Mountains*, obtainable from the BMC head office.

You can learn much from books, and you'll find a list of suggested further reading in Appendix 4, but there's no substitute for practical experience. One final repeat, though, of advice given throughout this book. Build up your skills and your equipment slowly; always beware of overstepping the limits of your ability; make a point of mastering each skill, rather than just bumbling around in the general direction at which this book aims you. Having done that, take CARE but don't take it all too seriously. Come on out and enjoy yourself!

Appendices

Appendix 1 Addresses

Organizations
The British Mountaineering Council
Crawford House, Precinct Centre, Manchester University, Booth Street East, Manchester 13

The Sports Council
70 Brompton Road, London SW3

The Backpacker's Club
Eric Gurney (National Organizer) 20 St Michael's Road, Tilehurst, Reading

The Camping Club of Great Britain and Ireland Ltd
11 Lower Grosvenor Place, London SW1

The Duke of Edinburgh's Award Scheme
Award Office, 2 Old Queen Street, London SW1

The Girl Guides Association
17–19 Buckingham Palace Road, London SW1

The Scout Association
25 Buckingham Palace Road, London SW1

The Ramblers Association
1–4 Crawford Mews, York Street, London W1H 1PT

The Youth Hostels Association
Trevelyan House, 8 St Stephen's Hill, St Alban's, Herts

The Outward Bound Trust
14 Oxford Street, London W1

Information services
The British Tourist Authority
64 St James Street, London SW1

The Countryside Commission
John Dower House, Crescent Place, Cheltenham, Gloucs

The Countryside Commission for Scotland
Battleby, Redgorton, Perth, Scotland

The Forestry Commission
25 Saville Row, London W1

The National Trust
42 Queen Anne's Gate, London SW1

The Mountain Rescue Committee
The Secretary, 9 Milldale Avenue, Temple Meads, Buxton,
Derbyshire SK17 9BE

Equipment suppliers (offering mail order service)
Black's of Greenock
Ruxley Corner, Sidcup, Kent DA4 5AQ

Ellis Brigham
6–14 Cathedral Street, Manchester M4 3FU

Field and Trek (Equipment) Ltd
23–5 Kings Road, Brentwood, Essex CM14 4ER

Pindisports
373 Uxbridge Road, Acton, London W3 9RH

Silvermans (government surplus)
2–8 Harford Street, London E1 4QD

Springlow Sales Ltd (expedition rations)
Marsland Industrial Estate, Werneth, Oldham, Lancs

National parks in England and Wales

Brecon Beacons	North Yorkshire Moors
Dartmoor	Peak District
Exmoor	Pembrokeshire Coast

| Lake District | Snowdonia |
| Northumberland | Yorkshire Dales |

Long-distance footpaths

Cleveland Way	Pennine Way
Cotswold Way	Ridgeway Path
North Downs Way	South Downs Way
Offa's Dyke Path	South West Peninsula Coast Path
Pembrokeshire Coast Path	Cambrian Way (still under negotiation)

Appendix 2 The Country Code

Guard against all risk of fire. Every year hundreds of hectares of countryside burn because of dropped matches, cigarette ends, even broken bottles focusing the sun's rays.

Fasten all gates. If animals are allowed to wander from where they've been put, they can ruin crops and endanger themselves, traffic and other people.

Keep dogs under proper control. Dogs, however docile, are instinctive hunters. If allowed to worry livestock they can kill – and cost you a great deal in fines. Keep them on a long lead if there's livestock about, and also on country lanes.

Keep to paths across farm land. Farm land is private, and if you wander off the right of way you're guilty of trespass. How would you like hordes of hikers tramping over your front lawn? Crops, including grass, can be damaged by inconsiderate people.

Avoid damaging fences, hedges and walls. They're vital to the farmer, expensive to mend and quite unnecessary to climb. There has to be a gate or stile somewhere; use it, and always shut gates after you.

Safegurad water supplies. This country is actually short of usable water. Don't pollute reservoir catchment areas, damage stream or river banks, or interfere with cattle troughs.

Protect wildlife, wild plants and trees. If everybody picks the primroses there won't be any left. Many plants are now very rare for just this reason. Observe the old adage, 'Take only photographs; leave only footprints'.

Go carefully on country roads. Blind corners, high banks and hedges, slow-moving farm machinery, animals and unmarked junctions all make country lanes dangerous. If you're driving, go slowly. If you're walking, keep to the right single file, to face oncoming traffic.

Respect the life of the countryside. Your playground is someone else's home, and livelihood. Try and fit in with the countryman's way of life and you'll help to preserve good relations as the countryside gets ever more crowded.

Appendix 3 Equipment lists

Day-trek
Small day-sack
Shell clothing
Hat, gloves and spare socks
Warm wear
Map, waterproofed, and routecard
Compass, watch and whistle
Notepad and ball-point pen
Space blanket or bivvy bag
Torch with spare battery
Rations, including hot drink
Problem pack and trail snacks
Any specialist gear required by conditions, eg rope, ice-axe, crampons

Camping expedition
For each individual, all the above items plus the following:
Rucksack
Sleeping-bag and ground insulation
Lightweight canteen
Spoon and cup
Knife

Headlamp with spare bulb and battery
Large polybag (eg dustbin liner)
Small towel and washing gear
Sun-tan cream, lipsalve and sunglasses
Emergency rations
Camp footwear

To be shared between occupants of each tent:
10m nylon cord
Toilet roll and trowel
Sponge (or two) for mopping up, cleaning tent, etc
Boot polish and rag
Stove
Matches, in waterproof container, or lighter with fuel
Fuel bottle, full
Windshield
Food box and water bottle
Tent lantern
Tent
Entertainment matter
First-aid kit

Clothing to be worn
Boots, with Vibram-type soles
Woollen socks, one or two pairs
Pants, and longjohns (winter) or shorts (summer)
Warm trousers (*not* jeans)
Vest and thin woollen sweater
Thicker woollen sweater, polo-necked
Woollen shirt or windproof jacket
Gaiters
Hat, gloves and shell clothing if appropriate

These are the items I carry, apart from special safety
equipment that I take when I'm in charge of a group. Your list
could well differ, depending on your style and scope of
expeditioning. Use this kit list purely as a starting point and
modify it continually.

Appendix 4 Suggested further reading

There are very many good books on the subject of expeditioning, or on specialized aspects of it. The following short list, though, will provide you with somewhere to start.

AA/Reader's Digest, *No Through Road*

Adshead, Robin, *Backpacking* (Spur Venture Guides, Spurbooks, 1977)

Balsillie, M. & Westwood, J., *Mid Moor and Mountain* (Scout Association, nd)

Blackshaw, Alan, *Mountaineering* (Kay & W, 1968; Penguin, 1970)

Booth, Derrick & Adshead, Robin, *Backpacking in Britain* (Oxford Illustrated Press, 1974)

Brown, Terence Henry & Hunter, R. H., *Camping* (Spur Venture Guides, Spurbooks, 1976)

——*Map and Compass* (Spur Venture Guides, Spurbooks, 1975)

——*Outdoor First Aid* (Spur Venture Guides, Spurbooks, 1975)

——*Survival and Rescue* (Spur Venture Guides, Spurbooks, nd)

——*Weather Lore* (Spur Venture Guides, Spurbooks, 1976)

Disley, John, *Expedition Guide* (Duke of Edinburgh's Award Office, nd)

Gardner, A. Ward & Roylance, Peter J., *New Essential First Aid* (Pan, 1972)

Jackson, John, *Safety on Mountains* (British Mountaineering Council, 1975)

Langmuir, Eric, *Mountain Leadership* (SCPR, nd)

Lumley, Peter, *Hill Trekking* (Spur Venture Guides, Spurbooks, 1976)

Scout Handbook (Scout Association, 1970)

Spur Footpath Guides (Spurbooks)

Sutton, O. G., *Understanding Weather* (Penguin, nd)

Journals

Camping and Outdoor Life (The Camping Club Journal)

Climber and Rambler (Holmes McDougall)

The Great Outdoors (Holmes McDougall)

Index

Numbers in *italic* type indicate illustrations.